COOL KNITS
FOR KIDS

25 stunning designs from baby to 7 years

Kate Gunn and Robyn Macdonald

hamlyn

An Hachette UK Company
www.hachette.co.uk

First published in Great Britain in 2007 by
Hamlyn, a division of Octopus Publishing Group Ltd
Endeavour House
189 Shaftesbury Avenue
London
WC2H 8JY
www.octopusbooks.co.uk

This edition published in 2011

ISBN: 978-0-600-62377-9

A CIP catalogue record for this book is available from
the British Library

Printed and bound in China

10 9 8 7 6 5 4 3 2 1

Note
Keep all small items used in the projects in this book,
such as buttons, out of reach of your children.

CONTENTS

knitting techniques

The designs in this book can be worked with a fairly basic knowledge of knitting. There is nothing super-difficult or excessively time consuming. Just read the instructions carefully, take your time and follow the useful tips given below.

Buttonholes

Knitting buttonholes can seem more complicated than it actually is, and full instructions are always given in your pattern instructions.

The simplest buttonholes are worked by making eyelet holes in the knitting with 'yarn overs'. Several of the cardigans in this book use this technique. A yarn over is made by looping the yarn over the right-hand needle to create a new stitch and a hole at the same time. The two stitches following the yarn over are knitted together to eliminate an extra stitch in the row. A buttonhole like this is complete in just one row.

The other most common method for buttonholes is worked over two rows as explained in the following steps.

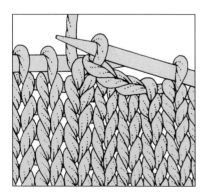

1 On the first row work to the position for the buttonhole. Cast/bind off the specified number of stitches. Work to the end.

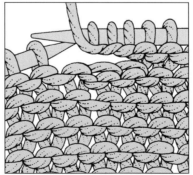

2 On the next row cast on the same number of stitches as were cast/bound off, using the single cast-on. This completes the buttonhole.

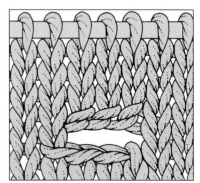

3 On the following row work into the back of the cast-on stitches for a neat finished effect.

Cables

Cables give bold sculptural texture to the knitted fabric. Once you learn the technique, cables are sure to become a firm favourite because of the beauty of the result (see the Cable Scarf on page 138 and the Cable and Lace Poncho on page 140).

If you have never tried cables before, use the instructions here to practise them. Cables vary in width, but the basic technique is the same: they twist either to the left or right depending on which side of the cable is in front of the other. The methods for both the right and the left twist are described below.

Cable 6 back

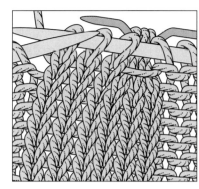 

1 Work to the position of the cable, slip the next three stitches onto the cable needle and hold them at the back of the work. Knit the next 3 stitches on the left-hand needle.

2 Next, knit the three stitches from the cable needle. On the next row, purl these stitches as usual. This cable coils to the right.

Cable 6 front

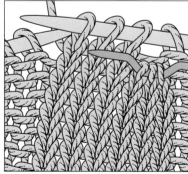 

1 Work to the position of the cable, slip the next three stitches onto the cable needle and hold them at the front of the work. Knit the next three stitches on the left-hand needle.

2 Next, knit the three stitches from the cable needle. On the next row, purl these stitches as usual. This cable coils to the left.

Knitting from a chart

Writing out a knitting pattern that has many colours in rows is very long-winded and difficult to follow. It is easier to visualize this type of knitting with the aid of a chart and to treat it as a picture, 'painting' with coloured yarns. Reading the chart is easier if you imagine it as the right side of a piece of knitting, working from the lower edge to the top. Each square on the chart represents one stitch; and each line of squares represents one row of knitting. When working from a knitting chart, read odd-numbered rows, 1, 3, 5, etc. (the right side of the fabric), from right to left, and even-numbered rows, 2, 4, 6, etc. (the wrong side of the fabric), from left to right. Each yarn colour used is given a letter in the pattern, which corresponds with a colour on the chart. This is shown in the key that accompanies the chart.

Fair Isle technique

Fair Isle knitting often uses many colours, but usually only two colours are used in each row. The colour not in use is stranded loosely across the back of the work until it is needed again. An easy way to deal with working with two colours in a row is to hold one yarn in your right hand and one in your left. With a little practice this will speed up your knitting.

Stranding yarn on a knit row

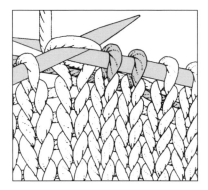 

1 On the row in which the second colour is introduced, join it at the right-hand edge. Begin knitting in the colour specified by the pattern or chart, carrying the other colour loosely across the back of the work.

2 To knit with the right-hand yarn, hold the left-hand yarn slightly under the needles. To knit with the left-hand yarn, hold the right-hand yarn out of the way.

Stranding on a purl row

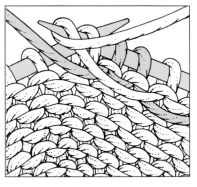 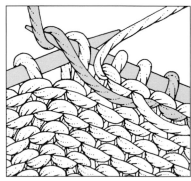

1 On the purl row the process is the same as for a knit row, except that the stranded yarn is held at the front of the work.

2 To purl with the right-hand yarn, hold the left-hand yarn under the needles. To purl with the left-hand yarn, hold the right-hand yarn out of the way.

Intarsia technique

The intarsia technique is used when a colour is used in an isolated area of the knitting (unlike with the Fair Isle technique, in which the colours are repeated all the way across the row). Because you may have several yarns on the go at the same time in intarsia knitting, you should use a separate length of yarn (or small ball) for each area of colour.

When you begin intarsia knitting, work in the first colour to the point for the colour change. If the second colour is being introduced for the first time, tie it securely to the first colour. On subsequent rows, twist the yarns together where they meet as explained here.

Changing colour on a knit row

When changing colour on a knit row, drop the first colour over the second, pick up the second colour and continue knitting with it. This twists the yarns around each other. If this were not done, the two areas of colour would be separate, leaving a split in the fabric.

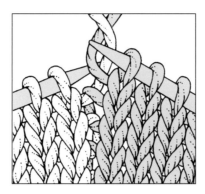

Changing colour on a purl row

When changing colour on a purl row, drop the first colour over the second, pick up the second and continue purling with it. On both knit and purl rows, work the stitches before and after the change fairly tightly to avoid leaving a gap.

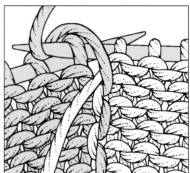

Finishing techniques

When you have spent many hours knitting, it is essential that you complete it correctly. Follow the simple instructions provided here to achieve a beautifully finished garment or accessory.

Blocking and pressing

It is important to block and press knitted garment pieces before sewing them together. This will help you shape the pieces to the correct size and give your knitting a professional-looking finish. With the wrong side of the fabric facing up, pin out each knitted piece onto an ironing board using the measurements given. Smoothing and stretching the pieces into shape like this is called 'blocking'.

If specific measurements are not provided for your project, pin out your knitting neatly without overstretching it and unfurl any edges that may be rolling up. Because each yarn is different, refer to the yarn label and press your knitted pieces according to manufacturer's instructions. Most of the yarns used in this book can be pressed. However, if your yarn contains acrylic, it may not be suitable for pressing, so check.

Always use a clean cloth between the knitting and your iron to avoid scorching. Then lightly press or steam the knitted fabric. Do not press down hard on the knitting and do not drag the iron over it; instead, lift the iron up and down when moving it to each new area. If you steam your knitting, remember to let it dry completely before removing the pins.

Weaving in ends

After blocking and pressing your finished pieces, you will need to sew in all the loose ends. Many knitters find this a very tedious task, but it is well worth putting in the effort.

Thread a blunt-ended yarn needle with the yarn end, weave the needle along about five stitches on the wrong side of the fabric and pull the thread through. Weave the needle in the opposite direction for about five stitches, pull the thread through and cut off the end of the yarn neatly, taking care that you do not snip through the stitches.

Sewing seams

After weaving in loose ends of yarn, you are ready to sew the seams on your knitting. Mattress stitch and backstitch are the two most widely used methods for joining together knitted pieces.

Mattress stitch is worked with the right sides of the knitted pieces facing you, and it is ideal for matching stripes accurately. For the best finish, mattress stitch should be worked one stitch in from the edge of the knitting.

Backstitch is worked with the right sides of the knitted pieces facing and produces a firm seam. Use a blunt-ended yarn needle for all seams.

Mattress stitch

With the right side of the knitting facing you, lay the pieces to be joined edge to edge. Insert the needle from the wrong side between the edge stitch and the second stitch. Take the yarn to the opposite piece, insert the needle from the front between the edge stitch and the second stitch, pass the needle under the loops of two rows and bring it back through to the front.

Insert the needle under the loops of the corresponding two rows in the opposite piece in the same way, and continue this zigzag lacing all along the seam.

Pull the yarn to close the seam, either after each action or after a few stitches. Do not to pull it too tight or leave it too loose, or the seam will pucker.

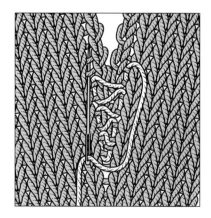

Backstitch

Pin the pieces to be joined with right sides together. Insert the needle into the knitting at the end, one stitch or row from the edge, then take the needle around the two edges to secure them and bring it back up through the fabric. Insert the needle into the fabric just behind where the previous stitch came out and make a short stitch.

Re-insert the needle where the previous stitch started and bring it up to make a longer stitch. Re-insert the needle where the previous stitch ended. Repeat to the end, taking care to match any pattern.

abbreviations

alt alternate

beg begin(ning)

C3B (cable 3 back) slip next st (P st) onto cable needle and hold at back of work, K2, then P1 from cable needle

C3F (cable 3 front) slip next 2 sts (K sts) onto cable needle and hold at front of work, P1, then K2 from cable needle

C4B (cable 4 back) slip next 2 sts onto cable needle and hold at back of work, K2, then K2 from cable needle

C4F (cable 4 front) slip next 2 sts onto cable needle and hold at front of work, K2, then K2 from cable needle

C5B (cable 5 back) slip next 3 sts (2 K sts and 1 P st) onto cable needle and hold at back of work, K2, then K2, P1 from cable needle

C8F (cable 8 front) slip next 4 sts onto cable needle and hold at front of work, K4, then K4 from cable needle

C10B (cable 10 back) slip next 5 sts onto cable needle and hold at back of work, K5, K5 from cable needle

C10F (cable 10 front) slip next 5 sts onto cable needle and hold at front of work, K5, then K5 from cable needle

cm centimetre(s)

cont continu(e)(ing)

dec decreas(e)(ing)

DK double knitting (a medium-weight yarn)

dvdec (double vertical decrease) insert right needle knitwise into first 2 sts on left needle and slip these 2 sts together onto right needle, knit next st, then insert left needle through 2 slipped sts and pass them over st just knit and off right needle (this decrease is worked over 3 sts and decreases 2 sts)

foll follow(s)(ing)

g gramme(s)

in inch(es)

inc increas(e)(ing)

K knit

K2tog knit next 2 sts together

K3tog knit next 3 sts together

mm millimetre(s)

oz ounce(s)

P purl

P2tog purl next 2 sts together

P3tog purl next 3 sts together

patt pattern

psso pass slipped stitch over

rem remain(s)(ing)

rep repeat(s)(ing)

rev st st (reverse stocking/stockinette stitch) purl sts on RS rows and knit sts on **WS** rows

RH right hand

RS right side

skp slip 1, knit 1, pass slipped stitch over stitch just knitted (one stitch de-creased)

sk2p slip 1, knit 2 together, pass slipped stitch over stitch just knitted together (2 stitches decreased)

st(s) stitch(es)

st st (stocking/stockinette stitch) knit sts on RS rows and purl sts on WS rows

tbl through back of loop(s)

WS wrong side

yf (yarn forward) bring yarn to front of work between needles and then over top of right needle to make a new stitch (US yarn over – yo)

TINY TOTS

alphabet patchwork blanket

This blanket is an ideal special present for any newborn baby. The letters and numbers are worked as separate patches, so you could personalize it to spell out the baby's name and birth date.

SIZE

Finished blanket measures approximately 79cm/31in square, including edging.

YARN

Rowan 4-Ply Cotton (50g/1¾oz per ball) as foll:

A pale blue-green/Ripple 121, 5 balls
B light blue/Bluebell 136, 2 balls
C beige/Opaque 112, 2 balls
NOTE: One ball is enough for six patches.

NEEDLES

Pair of 3mm (US size 3) knitting needles

TENSION/GAUGE

28 sts and 38 rows to 10cm/4in measured over st st using 3mm (US size 3) needles.

ABBREVIATIONS

See page 9.

CHART NOTE

Each of the 36 blanket patches is worked separately. Follow the chart and the chart key for each patch, working the letter or background in st st or rev st st as shown.

Read all odd-numbered (RS) chart rows from right to left and all even-numbered (WS) chart rows from left to right.

BLANKET PATCHES (make 36)

Using 3mm (US size 3) needles and yarn **A**, cast on 36 sts.

Foll chart for letter A and beg with chart row 1 (RS), work all 44 chart rows, ending with a WS row.

Cast/bind off.

Work rem 35 patches in same way, but using a different patch chart for each patch and yarn shades for each patch as foll:

Use yarn **A** for patches C, D, E, F, G, H, I, K, L, M, N, Q, T, U, V, X, Y, 0, 1, 2, 3, 6 and 8.

Use yarn **B** for patches B, P, R, W, 5 and 9.

Use yarn **C** for patches J, O, S, Z, 4 and 7.

EDGING STRIPS (make 4)

Using 3mm (US size 3) needles and yarn **B**, cast on 200 sts.

Work first edging strip in garter st (K every row) in stripes as foll:

Rows 1 and 2 Using yarn **B**, K into front and back of first st, K to last st, K into front and back of last st. 204 sts.

Rows 3 and 4 Using yarn **C**, rep rows 1 and 2. 208 sts.

Rows 5 and 6 Using yarn **A**, rep rows 1 and 2. 212 sts.

Rows 7–12 Rep rows 1–6. 224 sts.

Cast/bind off knitwise.

Work 3 more edging strips in same way.

TO FINISH

Press patches lightly on WS following instructions on yarn label. Do NOT press edging strips.

Starting at top of blanket, arrange 36 patches in 6 rows of 6 patches, organizing letters in alphabetical order and numbers after them, also in order, from 0 to 9.

Using mattress stitch, sew patches together in rows, then sew rows together.

Pin cast-on edge (shorter edge) of one edging strip to one side of blanket and sew in place.

Sew three remaining edging strips to other 3 sides of blanket in same way.

Sew together diagonal ends of edging strips at corners of blanket.

ALPHABET
PATCHWORK
BLANKET
CHART PATCHES

Chart key

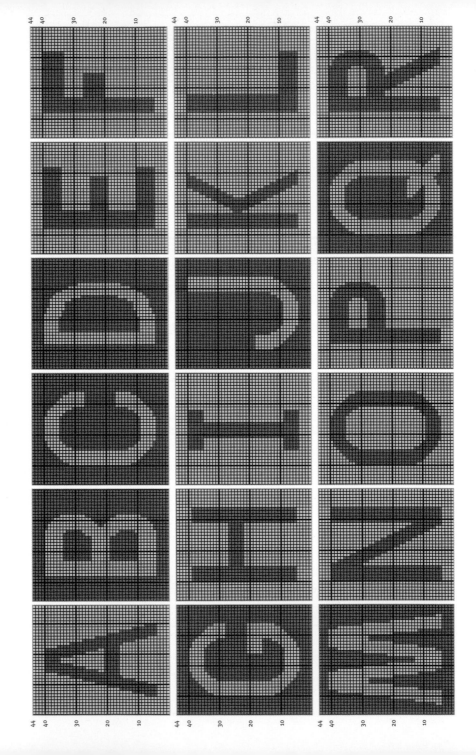

St St

Rev St St

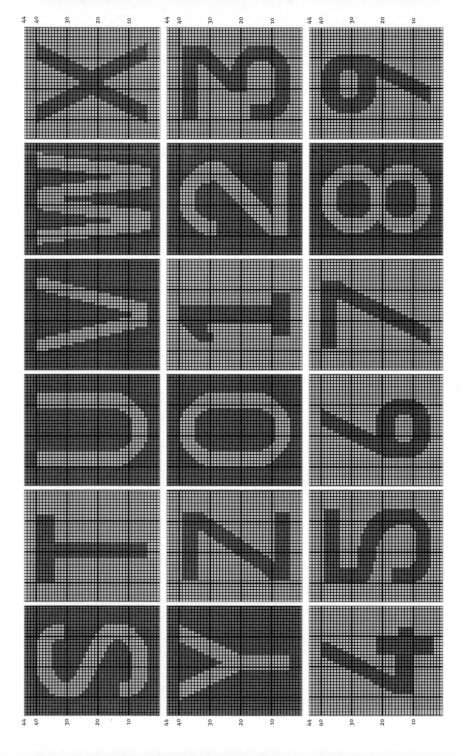

17

baby wrap cardigan

Wrap up baby in this chic cardigan, which is knitted in a luxurious wool-and-cotton yarn. Finished with a shiny satin ribbon, it is just right for wearing with party dresses.

SIZES & MEASUREMENTS

To fit

3–6	12–18	months

Knitted measurements

Around chest

46	54	cm
18	21¼	in

Length to shoulder

20	28	cm
8	11	in

Sleeve seam

14.5	16	cm
5¾	6¼	in

YARN

Two 50g/1¾oz balls of Rowan Soft Baby in lilac/Lizzy Lilac 010 or desired shade

NEEDLES & EXTRAS

Pair of 4½mm (US size 7) knitting needles
Pair of 4mm (US size 6) knitting needles
One small button
64cm/25in of 1.5cm/½in wide satin ribbon in a shade to match yarn

TENSION/GAUGE

20 sts and 28 rows to 10cm/4in measured over st st using 4½mm (US size 7) needles.

ABBREVIATIONS

See page 9.

BACK

Using 4½mm (US size 7) needles, cast on 49 (57) sts.

**Work 4 rows in garter st (K every row) for border.

Work 5 rows of lace patt as foll:

Row 1 (RS) K1, *yf, K2, sk2p, K2, yf, K1, rep from * to end.

Row 2 P to end.

Row 3 K2, *yf, K1, sk2p, k1, yf, K3, rep from *, ending last rep K2 instead of K3.

Row 4 P to end.

Row 5 K3, *yf, sk2p, yf, K5, rep from *, ending last rep K3 instead of K5.

This completes lace patt.**

Beg with a P row, work straight/even in st st for 25 (29) rows, ending with a WS row.

Shape armholes

Cont in st st throughout, work armhole shaping as foll:

Next row (RS) K3, skp, K39 (47), K2tog, K3. 47 (55) sts.

P 1 row.

Next row K3, skp, K37 (45), K2tog, K3. 45 (53) sts.

Work straight/even for 27 (31) rows, ending with a WS row.

Shape right neck edge and shoulder

Next row (RS) K11 (13), then turn, leaving rem sts on a stitch holder.

Work on these 11 (13) sts only for right side of neck.

Next row (WS) P2tog, P9 (11). 10 (12) sts.

Cast/bind off 5 (6) sts at beg of next row.

Cast/bind off rem 5 (6) sts.

Shape left neck edge and shoulder

With RS facing, rejoin yarn to sts on holder and cast/bind off centre 23 (27) sts, then K to end.

Next row (WS) P9 (11), P2tog. 10 (12) sts.

Cast/bind off 5 (6) sts at end of next row.

Rejoin yarn and cast/bind off rem 5 (6) sts.

LEFT FRONT

Using 4½ mm (US size 7) needles, cast on 41 (49) sts.

Work as for back from ** to **.

Beg with a P row, work straight/even in st st for 13 (17) rows, ending with a WS row.

Shape neck

Cont in st st throughout, beg neckline shaping as foll:

Next row (RS) K to last 5 sts, K2tog, K3.

Next row P3, P2tog, P to end.

Rep last 2 rows 5 times more. 29 (37) sts.

Shape armhole

Work armhole shaping and cont neckline shaping as foll:

Next row (RS) K3, skp, K19 (27), K2tog, K3. 27 (35) sts.

Next row P3, P2tog, P to end. 26 (34) sts.

Next row K3, skp, K16 (24), K2tog, K3. 24 (32) sts.

Next row P3, P2tog, P to end. 23 (31) sts.

Next row K to last 5 sts, K2tog, K3.

Next row P3, P2tog, P to end.

Rep last 2 rows 3 times more, ending with a WS row. 15 (23) sts.

Next row (RS) K to last 5 sts, K2tog, K3.

Next row P to end.

Rep last 2 rows 4 (10) times more, ending with a WS row. 10 (12) sts.

Work straight/even in st st for 10 (2) rows, ending with a WS row.

Shape shoulder

Cast/bind off 5 (6) sts at beg of next row.

Cast/bind off rem 5 (6) sts.

RIGHT FRONT

Using 4½ mm (US size 7) needles, cast on 41 (49) sts.

Work as for back from ** to **.

Beg with a P row, work straight/even in st st for 13 (17) rows, ending with a WS row.

Shape neck

Cont in st st throughout, beg neckline shaping as foll:

Next row (RS) K3, skp, K to end.

Next row P to last 5 sts, P2tog tbl, P3.

Rep last 2 rows 5 times more. 29 (37) sts.

Shape armhole

Work armhole shaping and cont neckline shaping as foll:

Next row (RS) K3, skp, K19 (27), K2tog, K3. 27 (35) sts.

Next row P to last 5 sts, P2tog tbl, P3. 26 (34) sts.

Next row K3, skp, K16 (24), K2tog, K3. 24 (32) sts.

Next row P to last 5 sts, P2tog tbl, P3. 23 (31) sts.

Next row (RS) K3, skp, K to end.

Next row P to last 5 sts, P2tog tbl, P3.

Rep last 2 row 3 times more, ending with a WS row. 15 (23) sts.

Next row (RS) K3, skp, K to end.

Next row P to end.

Rep last 2 rows 4 (10) times more. 10 (12) sts.

Work straight/even in st st for 10 (2) rows, ending with a WS row.

Shape shoulder

Cast/bind off 5 (6) sts at end of next row.

Rejoin yarn and cast/bind off rem 5 (6) sts.

SLEEVES (make 2)

Using 4½mm (US size 7) needles, cast on 25 (33) sts.

Work as for back from ** to **.

Beg with a P row, work straight/even in st st for 3 rows, ending with a WS row.

Cont in st st throughout, inc 1 st at each end of next row and then every 3rd (4th) row 6 times, ending with a RS row. 39 (47) sts.

Work straight/even for 3 rows, ending with a WS row.

Shape top of sleeve

Next row (RS) K3, skp, K to last 5 sts, K2tog, K3.

Next row P to end.

Rep last 2 rows once more, ending with a WS row. 35 (43) sts.

Cast/bind off 3 sts at beg of next 10 (12) rows.

Cast/bind off rem 5 (7) sts.

EDGING

Using 4mm (US size 6) needles, cast on 151 (171) sts.

Row 1 (RS) K1, *yf, K2tog, rep from * to end.

Row 2 P to end.

Row 3 P to end.

Row 4 P to end.

Row 5 K14 (18), K3tog, K44 (48), K3tog, K23 (27), K3tog, K44 (48), K3tog, K14 (18). 143 (163) sts.

Row 6 P to end.

Cast/bind off.

TO FINISH

Press pieces lightly on WS following instructions on yarn label.

Sew both shoulder seams.

Pin cast/bound-off edge of edging in position along front edges and back neck, with curved corners of edging aligned with shoulder seams and front shaping. Sew edging in place. Fold top of each sleeve in half to find centre and mark with a pin. Sew sleeves to armholes, matching centre of top of sleeve to shoulder seam.

Sew right side seam and sleeve seam. Then sew a button to WS of right side seam 10cm/4in up from cast-on edge (eyelet holes on left front edging will serve as buttonholes). Cut ribbon in half and sew one length to side edge of left front so that centre of ribbon is 9cm/3½in up from cast-on edge and so that ribbon can be caught in seam. Sew left side seam and sleeve seam.

Sew second length of ribbon to WS of edging seam on right front so that it matches position of ribbon on left front.

Tie ribbons in a bow to fasten cardigan.

sandal bootees

These cute booties will look great with a pretty dress for special occasions. There is enough yarn to make mittens as well – just follow the instructions on page 34, omitting the stripes.

SIZE
One size to fit 0–6 months

YARN
One 50g/1³⁄₄oz ball of Rowan 4-Ply Cotton in light pink/Orchid 120 or desired shade

NEEDLES & EXTRAS
Pair of 3mm (US size 3) needles
2 small buttons

TENSION/GAUGE
28 sts and 38 rows to 10cm/4in measured over st st using 3mm (US size 3) needles.

ABBREVIATIONS
See page 9.

SOLES (make 2)

Using 3mm (US size 3) needles, cast on 8 sts.
Work sole in moss/seed st as foll:

Row 1 *K1, P1, rep from * to end.

Row 2 K into front and back of first st, *K1, P1, rep from * to last st, K into front and back of last st. 10 sts.

Row 3 Rep row 2. 12 sts.

Row 4 *P1, K1, rep from * to end.

Row 5 K into front and back of first st, *P1, K1, rep from * to last st, K into front and back of last st. 14 sts.

Rows 6 and 7 Rep rows 1 and 2. 16 sts.

Rows 8 and 9 Rep rows 4 and 5. 18 sts.

Row 10 *K1, P1, rep from * to end.

Row 11 *P1, K1, rep from * to end.

Rows 12–31 Rep rows 10 and 11 ten times.

Row 32 P2tog, *K1, P1, rep from * to last 2 sts, K2tog. 16 sts.

Row 33 Rep row 10.

Row 34 K2tog, *P1, K1, rep from * to last 2 sts, P2tog. 14 sts.

Row 35 Rep row 11.

Rows 36–38 Rep rows 32–34. 10 sts.

Row 39 Rep row 34. 8 sts.

Row 40 Rep row 11.

Cast/bind off in moss/seed st.

TOPS OF BOOTEE (make 2)

Using 3mm (US size 3) needles, cast on 70 sts.

Rows 1 and 2 K to end.

Row 3 (RS) K28, dvdec, K8, dvdec, K28. 66 sts.

Row 4 (WS) P to end.

Row 5 K26, dvdec, K8, dvdec, K26. 62 sts.

Row 6 P to end.

Row 7 K23, dvdec, K10, dvdec, K23. 58 sts.

Row 8 K to end.

Row 9 K21, dvdec, K1, [yf, K2tog] 4 times, K1, dvdec, K21. 54 sts.

Row 10 K to end.

Row 11 K19, dvdec, K10, dvdec, K19. 50 sts.

Row 12 V K17, P16, K17.

Row 13 K17, dvdec, K10, dvdec, K17. 46 sts.

Row 14 K17, P12, K17.

Cast/bind off firmly knitwise.

STRAPS (make 2)

Using 3mm (US size 3) needles, cast on 20 sts.

Rows 1 and 2 K to end.

Row 3 K1, [yf, K2tog] 9 times, K1.

Rows 4 and 5 K to end.

Cast/bind off purlwise.

TO FINISH

Do NOT press pieces.

Sew together row-end edges of each top of bootee to form heel seam. Sew cast-on edge of each top to a sole.

Sew one strap to inner side of each bootee as shown. Sew one button to outer side of each bootee. (Make sure when attaching straps and buttons that second bootee is mirror image of first.) Eyelet holes on strap serve as buttonholes, so strap length can be adjusted to fit.

baby hoodie

For a stylish, up-to-date cover-up, knit baby this raglan-sleeved sweater with attached hood. There are simple instructions for four different sizes, to fit from a newborn to a two-year-old.

SIZES & MEASUREMENTS

To fit

0–3 months	3–6	6–12	12–24	

Knitted measurements

Around chest

46	50	54	58	cm
18	19³⁄₄	21¹⁄₄	22³⁄₄	in

Length to shoulder

24	26	28	30	cm
9¹⁄₂	10¹⁄₄	11	11³⁄₄	in

Sleeve seam

16	18	19	21	cm
6¹⁄₄	7	7¹⁄₂	8¹⁄₄	in

YARN

3 (4: 4: 4) 50g/1³⁄₄oz balls of Jaeger Baby Merino DK in blue/Ocean 226 or desired shade

NEEDLES

Pair of 3³⁄₄mm (US size 5) knitting needles
Pair of 4mm (US size 6) knitting needles

TENSION/GAUGE

22 sts and 30 rows to 10cm/4in measured over st st using 4mm (US size 6) needles.

ABBREVIATIONS

See page 9.

BACK

Using 3¾mm (US size 5) needles, cast on 52 (56: 60: 64) sts.

Rib row 1 (RS) *K2, P2, rep from * to end.

Rep last row 7 times more, ending with a WS row.

Change to 4mm (US size 6) needles.

Beg with a K row, work 34 (38: 42: 46) rows in st st, ending with a WS row.

Shape raglan armholes

Cont in st st throughout, beg armhole shaping as foll:

Next row (dec row) (RS) K3, skp, K to last 5 sts, K2tog, K3.

Next row P to end.

Rep last 2 rows 3 (4: 5: 6) times more, ending with a WS row. 44 (46: 48: 50) sts.

Work straight/even for 2 rows, ending with a WS row.

Rep raglan dec row. 42 (44: 46: 48) sts.**

***Work straight/even for 3 rows, ending with a WS row.

Rep raglan dec row.***

Rep from *** to *** twice more. 36 (38: 40: 42) sts.

Work straight/even for 3 rows, ending with a WS row.

Shape right neck edge and shoulder

Next row (RS) K2tog, K7, then turn, leaving rem 27 (29: 31: 33) sts on a stitch holder.

Work on these 8 sts only for right side of neck.

Next row (WS) P2tog, P to end.

Next row K to last 2 sts, K2tog.

Rep last 2 rows once more. 4 sts.

Purl 1 row.

Cast/bind off.

Shape left neck edge and shoulder

With RS facing, rejoin yarn to sts on holder and cast/bind off centre 18 (20: 22: 24) sts, then K to last 2 sts, K2tog. 8 sts.

Next row (WS) P to last 2 sts, P2tog.

Next row K2tog, K to end.

Rep last 2 rows once more. 4 sts.

Purl 1 row.

Cast/bind off.

FRONT

Work as for back to **.

Work straight/even for 3 rows, ending with a WS row.

Next row (RS) K3, skp, K to last 5 sts. K2tog, K3. 40 (42: 44: 46) sts.

P 1 row.

Shape left neck edge and shoulder

Next row (RS) K16, then turn, leaving rem 24 (26: 28: 30) sts on a stitch holder.

Work on these 16 sts only for left side of neck.

Next row (WS) P2tog, P14. 15 sts.

Next row K3, skp, K8, K2tog. 13 sts.

Next row P2tog, P11. 12 sts.

Next row K10, K2tog. 11 sts.

Purl 1 row.

Next row K3, skp, K4, K2tog. 9 sts.

Purl 1 row.

Next row K7, K2tog. 8 sts.

Purl 1 row.

Next row K2tog, K4, K2tog. 6 sts.

Purl 1 row.

Next row K to last 2 sts, K2tog.

Rep last 2 rows once more. 4 sts.

Purl 1 row.

Cast/bind off.

Shape right neck edge and shoulder

With RS facing, rejoin yarn to sts on holder and cast/bind off centre 8 (10: 12: 14) sts, then K to end. 16 sts.

Next row (WS) P14, P2tog. 15 sts.

Next row K2tog, K8, K2tog, K3. 13 sts.

Next row P11, P2tog. 12 sts.

Next row K2tog, K10. 11 sts.

Purl 1 row.

Next row K2tog, K4, K2tog, K3. 9 sts.

Purl 1 row.

Next row K2tog, K7. 8 sts.

Purl 1 row.

Next row K2tog, K4, K2tog. 6 sts.

Purl 1 row.

Next row K2tog, K to end.

Rep last 2 rows once more. 4 sts.

Purl 1 row.

Cast/bind off.

SLEEVES (make 2)

Using 3¾mm (US size 5) needles, cast on 26 (28: 30: 32) sts.

Rib row 1 (RS) K2 (1: 2: 1), *P2, K2, rep from * to last 4 (3: 4: 3) sts, P2, K2 (1: 2: 1)

Rib row 2 (WS) P2 (1: 2: 1), *K2, P2, rep from * to last 4 (3: 4: 3) sts, K2, P2 (1: 2: 1)

Rep last 2 rows 3 times more.

Change to 4mm (US size 6) needles.

Beg with a K row, work 2 rows in st st, ending with a WS row.

Cont in st st throughout, inc 1 st at each end of next row and then every foll 6th row until there are 40 (44: 48: 52) sts, ending with a RS row.

Work straight/even for 3 (3: 1: 1) rows, ending with a WS row.

Shape raglan top of sleeve

Next row (RS) K3, skp, K to last 5 sts, K2tog, K3.

Next row P to end.

Rep last 2 rows 10 times more, ending with a WS row.

Next row (RS) Skp, K to last 2 sts, K2tog.

Next row P to end.

Rep last 2 rows until 8 (10: 12: 14) sts rem, ending with a WS row.

Cast/bind off.

LEFT SIDE OF HOOD

Using 4mm (US size 6) needles, cast on 49 (53: 57: 61) sts.

Beg with a K row, work 4 (6: 8: 10) rows in st st, ending with a WS row.

Shape hood

Cont in st st throughout, shape hood as foll:

Next row (RS) K2tog, K to end.

Next row P to last 2 sts, P2tog.

Rep last two rows 4 times more. 39 (43: 47: 51) sts.

Next row (RS) K to last 5 sts, K2tog, K3.

Next row P to end.

Rep last two rows 10 times more. 28 (32: 36: 40) sts.

Next row (RS) K2tog, K to last 5 sts, K2tog, K3.

Next row P to last 2 sts, P2tog.

Rep last 2 rows twice more. 19 (23: 27: 31) sts.

Cast/bind off 3 sts at beg of next 4 (6: 6: 8) rows.

Cast/bind off rem 7 (5: 9: 7) sts.

RIGHT SIDE OF HOOD

Using 4mm (US size 6) needles, cast on 49
(53: 57: 61) sts.

Beg with a K row, work 4 (6: 8: 10) rows in st
st, ending with a WS row.

Shape hood

Cont in st st throughout, shape hood as foll:

Next row (RS) K to last 2 sts, K2tog.

Next row P2tog, P to end.

Rep last two rows 4 times more. 39 (43: 47:
51) sts.

Next row (RS) K3, skp, K to end.

Next row P to end.

Rep last two rows 10 times more. 28 (32: 36:
40) sts.

Next row (RS) K3, skp, K to last 2 sts, K2tog.

Next row P2tog, P to end.

Rep last 2 rows twice more. 19 (23: 27: 31) sts.

Cast/bind off 3 sts at beg of next 4 (6: 6: 8)
rows.

Cast/bind off rem 7 (5: 9: 7) sts.

HOOD EDGING

Using 3¾mm (US size 5) needles, cast on 98
(106: 114: 122) sts.

Rib row 1 (RS) *K2, P2, rep from * to last 2 sts,
K2.

Rib row 2 (WS) *P2, K2, rep from * to last 2
sts, P2.

Rep last 2 rows 1 (1: 2: 2) times more.

Cast/bind off in rib.

TO FINISH

Press pieces lightly on WS following instructions
on yarn label and avoiding ribbing.

Weave in all loose ends.

Sew raglan seams.

Pin hood pieces together and sew centre back
seam along edge with decorative decreases
and cast/bound-off sts.

Sew hood edging to cast-on edges of hood.

Then leaving ribbed edge of hood free, sew
remaining edge to neck edge of sweater.

Sew side and sleeve seams.

stripy bootees and mittens

These bootees and mittens will keep delicate fingers and toes cosy. Made from soft cotton yarn, they are quick and easy to knit. Try them in different shades to match favourite outfits.

SIZE
One size to fit 0–6 months

YARN
Bootees
Rowan 4-Ply Cotton (50g/1¾oz) balls as foll:
A green/Fennel 135, 1 ball
B turquoise blue/Aegean 129, 1 ball
C pale yellow/Honey Dew 140, 1 ball
Mittens
Rowan 4-Ply Cotton (50g/1¾oz) balls as foll:
A green/Fennel 135, 1 ball
B turquoise blue/Aegean 129, 1 ball
C pale yellow/Honey Dew 140, 1 ball
NOTE: If you are making both bootees and mittens, one ball in each shade is enough for both.

NEEDLES & EXTRAS
Pair of 3mm (US size 3) knitting needles
Bootees only: 3mm (US size D/3) crochet
   hook and 2 small buttons

TENSION/GAUGE
28 sts and 38 rows to 10cm/4in measured over st st using 3mm (US size 3) needles.

ABBREVIATIONS
See page 9.

BOOTEES

Soles (make 2)

Using 3mm (US size 3) needles and yarn **A**, cast on 9 sts.

Work in garter st (K every row) in 2-row yarn **A**, 2-row yarn **B** stripe patt as foll:

Row 1 (RS) Using yarn **A**, K to end.

Row 2 Using yarn **A**, K to end.

Row 3 Using yarn **B**, K into front and back of first st, K to last st, K into front and back of last st. 11 sts.

Row 4 Using yarn **B**, K to end.

Cont in 4-row garter st stripe patt (2 rows **A**, 2 rows **B**) as set throughout, inc 1 st at each end of next row and foll alt row. 15 sts.

Work straight/even for 3 rows.

Inc 1 st at each end of next row. 17 sts.

Work straight/even for 29 rows.

Dec 1 st at each end of next row and then 3 foll alt rows. 9 sts.

Work straight/even for 1 row.

Cast/bind off knitwise.

Top of bootee – side A (make 2)

Using 3mm (US size 3) needles and yarn **A**, cast on 66 sts.

Work in st st in 2-row yarn **A**, 2-row yarn **B** stripes as foll:

Row 1 (RS) Using yarn **A**, K to end.

Row 2 Using yarn **A**, P to end.

Row 3 Using yarn B, K14, dvdec, K17, dvdec, K29. 62 sts.

Row 4 Using yarn **B**, P to end.

Row 5 Using yarn **A**, K13, dvdec, K15, dvdec, K28. 58 sts.

Row 6 Using yarn **A**, P to end.

Row 7 Using yarn **B**, K12, dvdec, K13, dvdec, K27. 54 sts.

Row 8 Using yarn **B**, P to end.

Row 9 Using yarn **A**, K2tog, K9, dvdec, K11, dvdec, K26. 49 sts.

Row 10 Using yarn **A**, K15, P32, P2tog. 48 sts.

Row 11 Using yarn **B**, K2tog, K6, dvdec, K9, dvdec, K25. 43 sts.

Row 12 Using yarn **B**, K15, P26, P2tog. 42 sts.

Row 13 Using yarn **A**, K2tog, K3, [dvdec, K2] twice, dvdec, K24. 35 sts.

Row 14 Using yarn **A**, K15, P18, P2tog. 34 sts.

Row 15 Using yarn **B**, K2tog, [dvdec] 3 times, K23. 27 sts.

Row 16 Using yarn **B**, K15, P12.

Break off yarns **A** and **B**.

Edging

Work edging as foll:

Row 17 (RS) Join in yarn **C** and pick up and knit 14 sts along right edge of knitting, then knit across 27 sts on needle. 41 sts.

Row 18 K23, K3tog, K15. 39 sts.

Cast off/bind off knitwise.

Top of bootee – side B (make 2)

Using 3mm (US size 3) needles and yarn **A**, cast on 66 sts.

Work in st st in 2-row yarn **A**, 2-row yarn **B** stripes as foll:

Row 1 (RS) Using yarn **A**, K to end.

Row 2 Using yarn **A**, P to end.

Row 3 Using yarn **B**, K29, dvdec, K17, dvdec, K14. 62 sts.

Row 4 Using yarn **B**, P to end.

Row 5 Using yarn **A**, K28, dvdec, K15, dvdec, K13. 58 sts.

Row 6 Using yarn **A**, P to end.

Row 7 Using yarn **B**, K27, dvdec, K13, dvdec, K12. 54 sts.

Row 8 Using yarn **B**, P to end.

Row 9 Using yarn **A**, K26, dvdec, K11, dvdec, K9, K2tog. 49 sts.

Row 10 Using yarn **A**, P2tog, p32, K15. 48 sts.

Row 11 Using yarn **B**, K25, dvdec, K9, dvdec, K6, K2tog. 43 sts.

Row 12 Using yarn **B**, P2tog, P26, K15. 42 sts.

Row 13 Using yarn **A**, K24, [dvdec, K2] twice, dvdec, K3, K2tog. 35 sts.

Row 14 Using yarn **A**, P2tog, P18, K15. 34sts.

Row 15 Using yarn **B**, K23, [dvdec] 3 times, K2tog. 27 sts.

Row 16 Using yarn **B**, P12, K15.

Edging

Work edging as foll:

Row 17 (RS) Join in yarn **C** and K 27 sts on needle, then with RS still facing, pick up and knit 14 sts along left edge of knitting. 41 sts.

Row 18 K15, K3tog, K23. 39 sts.

Cast/bind off knitwise.

TO FINISH

Sew longest edge of one side A to longest edge of one side B to form heel seam. Sew together remaining side A and side B in the same way.

Place soles so that right sides of knitting are face down – cast-on edge is at heel and the cast/bound-off edge is at toe. Then pin tops of bootees to soles, positioning heel seam at centre of back of the sole – one side will over-lap other side at toe. (Make sure that left-foot bootee is mirror image of right-foot bootee.)

Using a blunt-ended yarn needle and yarn **C**, blanket stitch tops to the soles.

Using 3mm (US size D/3) crochet hook, make 8 chain stitches for buttonhole loop and fasten off (adjust length if necessary to suit button). Sew chain loop to outer side of top of one bootee.

Make a second buttonhole loop in same way and sew to second bootee.

Sew on buttons to correspond with button-hole loops.

MITTENS

To make mittens

The mittens have no thumbs and are identical.

Using 3mm (US size 3) needles and yarn **C**, cast on 36 sts.

Rib row 1 *K1, P1, rep from * to end.

Rep last row 7 times more.

Break off yarn **C**.

Beg st st stripe patt as foll:

Row 1 (RS) Using yarn **B**, K to end.

Row 2 Using yarn **B**, P to end.

Row 3 Using yarn **A**, K to end.

Row 4 Using yarn **A**, P to end.

Beg with a K row, cont in st st working in stripes as foll:

Work [2 rows yarn **B**, 2 rows yarn **A**] 3 times, 2 rows yarn **C**, 2 rows yarn **A**.

Shape top of mitten

Shape top of mitten in stripes as foll:

Next row (RS) Using yarn **B**, [K2, skp, K11, K2tog] twice, K2. 32 sts.

Using yarn **B**, P 1 row.

Break off yarns **A** and **B** and cont with yarn C only.

Next row [K2, skp, K9, K2tog] twice, K2. 28 sts.

P 1 row.

Next row [K2, skp, K7, K2tog] twice, K2. 24 sts.

P 1 row.

Cast/bind off.

Make second mitten in exactly same way.

TO FINISH

Sew seam on each mitten, matching stripes carefully.

pointy hat

This pointy hat is worked in two-row stripes in a soft mercerized cotton yarn. If the tiny tot likes it, you can make several in various stripe combinations in no time at all.

SIZES

To fit

0–3	3–6	6–12	12–24

months

YARN

Jaeger Aqua (50g/1¾oz per ball) as foll:
A bright pink/India 322, 1 ball
B dark purple/Deep 320, 1 ball
C light green/Herb 303, 1 ball

NEEDLES

Pair of 3¾mm (US size 5) knitting needles
Pair of 4mm (US size 6) knitting needles

TENSION/GAUGE

22 sts and 30 rows to 10cm/4in measured over st st using 4mm (US size 6) needles.

ABBREVIATIONS

See page 9.

TO MAKE HAT

Using 3¾mm (US size 5) needles and yarn **C**, cast on 68 (72: 76: 80) sts.

Rib row 1 (RS) *K2, P2, rep from * to end.

Rep last row 5 times more, ending with a WS row.

Change to 4mm (US size 6) needles.

Begin stripe pattern

Beg st st stripe patt as foll:

Row 1 (RS) Using yarn **A**, K to end.

Row 2 Using yarn **A**, P to end.

Row 3 Using yarn **B**, K to end.

Row 4 Using yarn **B**, P to end.

Rep last 4 rows 1 (2: 3: 4) more times.

Beg with a K row and cont in st st, 2 rows yarn **C**, [2 rows in yarn **B**, 2 rows yarn **A**] twice, and 2 rows yarn **C**, ending with a WS row.

Shape top of hat

Shape top of hat as foll:

Row 1 (RS) Using yarn **A**, K7 (7 : 8: 8), [dvdec, K14 (15: 16: 17)] 3 times, dvdec, K7 (8: 8: 9). 60 (64: 68: 72) sts.

Row 2 Using **A**, P to end.

Row 3 Using yarn **B**, K to end.

Row 4 Using yarn **B**, P to end.

Row 5 Using yarn **A**, K6 (6: 7: 7), [dvdec, K12 (13: 14: 15)] 3 times, dvdec, K6 (7: 7: 8). 52 (56: 60: 64) sts.

Row 6 Using yarn **A**, P to end.

Row 7 Using yarn **B**, K to end.

Row 8 Using yarn **B**, P to end.

Row 9 Using yarn A, K5 (5: 6: 6), [dvdec, K10 (11: 12: 13)] 3 times, dvdec, K5 (6: 6: 7). 44 (48: 52: 56) sts.

Row 10 Using yarn **A**, P to end.

Row 11 Using yarn **B**, K4 (4: 5: 5), [dvdec, K8 (9: 10: 11)] 3 times, dvdec, K4 (5: 5: 6). 36 (40: 44: 48) sts.

Row 12 Using yarn **B**, P to end.

Row 13 Using yarn **C**, K3 (3: 4: 4), [dvdec, K6 (7: 8: 9)] 3 times, dvdec, K3 (4: 4: 5). 28 (32: 36: 40) sts.

Row 14 Using yarn **C**, P to end.

Row 15 Using yarn **B**, K2 (2: 3: 3), [dvdec, K4 (5: 6: 7)] 3 times, dvdec, K2 (3: 3: 4). 20 (24: 28: 32) sts.

Row 16 Using yarn **B**, P to end.

Row 17 Using yarn **A**, K to end.

Row 18 Using yarn **A**, P to end.

Break off yarn **A**.

Row 19 Using yarn **B**, K1 (1: 2: 2), [dvdec, K2 (3: 4: 5)] 3 times, dvdec, K1 (2: 2: 3). 12 (16: 20: 24) sts.

Row 20 Using yarn **B**, P to end.

Break off yarn **B** and cont with yarn **C** only.

Row 21 K0 (0: 1: 1), [dvdec, K0 (1: 2: 3)] 3 times, dvdec, K0 (1: 1: 2). 4 (8: 12: 16) sts.

For sizes 3–6, 6–12 and 12–24 months only

Row 22 P to end.

Row 23 *K2tog, rep from * to end. – (4: 6: 8) sts.

For all sizes

Leaving rem 4 (4: 6: 8) sts on needle, break off yarn, leaving a long tail-end to sew hat seam.

TO FINISH

Thread end of yarn onto yarn needle and pass needle through remaining stitches while slipping them off knitting needle. Pull yarn to gather stitches and secure, then sew hat seam using mattress stitch.

stripy sweater

A stripy sweater knitted in smooth cotton is a good option for a baby with skin too sensitive for wool. Pick your favourite shades for the stripes and pair the finished sweater with casual wear.

SIZES & MEASUREMENTS
To fit

3–6	6–12	12–24	months

Knitted measurements

Around chest

52	58	64	cm
20½	22¾	25¼	in

Length to shoulder

27	30	32	cm
10¾	11¾	12¾	in

Sleeve seam

20	22	24	cm
8	8¾	9½	in

YARN
Rowan Handknit Cotton (50g/1¾oz per ball) as foll:

A cream/Ecru 251, 3 balls
B brown/Double Choc 315, 3 balls
C green/Gooseberry 219, 1 ball

NEEDLES & EXTRAS
Pair of 4mm (US size 6) knitting needles
Pair of 4½mm (US size 7) knitting needles
4 small buttons

TENSION/GAUGE
20 sts and 28 rows to 10cm/4in measured over st st using 4½mm (US size 7) needles.

ABBREVIATIONS
See page 9.

CHART NOTE
Work the stripe chart pattern in stocking/stockinette stitch. Read all odd-numbered (knit) chart rows from right to left and all even-numbered (purl) chart rows from left to right.

BACK

Using 4mm (US size 6) needles and yarn **C**, cast on 52 (58: 64) sts.

Rib row 1 (RS) K1 (2: 1), *P2, K2, rep from * to last 3 (4: 3) sts, P2, K1 (2: 1).

Rib row 2 (WS) P1 (2: 1), *K2, P2, rep from * to last 3 (4: 3) sts, K2, P1 (2: 1).

Break off yarn **C**.

Using yarn **B**, rep rib rows 1 and 2 twice.

Using yarn **A**, rep rib rows 1 and 2 twice.**

Change to 4½mm (US size 7) needles.

Beg with a K row (chart row 1), work stripe chart patt in st st – between markers for chosen size – until chart row 61 (65: 69) has been completed, ending with a RS row.

Shape left shoulder

Cont in st st and foll chart for stripes through-out, cast/bind off 3 (4 : 4) sts at beg of next row. 49 (54: 60) sts.

Work straight/even for 1 row.

Cast/bind off 3 (3: 4) sts at beg of next row, ending with a WS row. 46 (51: 56) sts.

Shape right neck edge and shoulder

Next row (RS) Cast/bind off first 3 (4: 4) sts, K until there are 13 (14: 16) sts on right needle, then turn, leaving rem sts on a stitch holder. Work on these 13 (14: 16) sts only for right side of neck.

Dec 1 st at beg of next row (neck edge). 12 (13: 15) sts.

Next row (RS) Cast/bind off first 3 (3: 4) sts, K to last 2 sts, K2tog. 8 (9: 10) sts.

Work straight/even for 1 row.

Cast/bind off 3 (3: 4) sts at beg of next row and then 3 sts at beg of foll alt row.

Work straight/even for 1 row.

Cast/bind off rem 2 (3: 3) sts.

Shape left neck edge

With RS facing, rejoin yarn to sts on holder and cast/bind off centre 20 (22: 24) sts, then K to end. 10 (11: 12) sts.

Next row (WS) Cast/bind off first 3 (3: 4) sts, P to last 2 sts, P2tog. 6 (7: 7) sts.

Dec 1 st at beg of next row. 5 (6: 6) sts.

Cast/bind off 3 sts at beg of next row.

Work straight/even for 1 row.

Cast/bind off rem 2 (3: 3) sts.

FRONT

Work as for back to **.

Change to 4½mm (US size 7) needles.

Beg with a K row (chart row 1), work stripe chart patt in st st – between markers for chosen size – until chart row 60 (64: 68) has been completed, ending with a WS row.

Shape left neck edge and shoulder

Cont in st st and foll chart for stripes through-out, shape left neck edge and shoulder as foll:

Next row (RS) Cast/bind off first 3 (4: 4) sts, K until there 18 (19: 21) sts on right needle, then turn, leaving rem sts on a stitch holder. Work on these 18 (19: 21) sts only for left side of neck.

Dec 1 st at beg of next row (neck edge). 17 (18: 20) sts.

Next row (RS) Cast/bind off first 3 (3: 4) sts, K to last 2 sts, K2tog.

Dec 1 st at beg of next row (neck edge).

Rep last 2 rows once more. 7 (8: 8) sts.

Next row (RS) Cast/bind off first 3 sts, K to last 2 sts, K2tog. 3 (4: 4) sts.

Dec 1 st at beg of next row (neck edge).

Cast/bind off rem 2 (3: 3) sts.

Shape right neck edge and shoulder

With RS facing, rejoin yarn to sts on holder and cast/bind off centre 10 (12: 14) sts, then K to end. 21 (23: 25) sts.

Dec 1 st at end of next row (neck) edge.

Dec 1 st at beg of next row.

Rep last 2 rows once more. 17 (19: 21) sts.

Next row (WS) Cast/bind off first 3 (4: 4) sts, P to last 2 sts, P2tog. 13 (14: 16) sts.

Dec 1 st at beg of next row. 12 (13: 15) sts.

Next row (WS) Cast/bind off first 3 (3: 4) sts, P to last 2 sts, P2tog. 8 (9: 10) sts.

Next row (RS) K to end.

Next row (WS) Cast/bind off first 3 (3: 4) sts, P to end. (5: 6: 6) sts.

Next row (RS) K to end.

Next row (WS) Cast/bind off first 3 sts, P to end. Cast/bind off rem 2 (3: 3) sts.

SLEEVES (make 2)

Using 4mm (US size 6) needles and yarn C, cast on 26 (30: 34) sts.

Rib row 1 (RS) *K2, P2, rep from * to last 2 sts, K2.

Rib row 2 *P2, K2, rep from * to last 2 sts, P2. Break off yarn **C**.

Using yarn **B**, rep rib rows 1 and 2 twice.

Using yarn **A**, rep rib rows 1 and 2 twice and inc 1 st at each end of last row. 28 (32: 36) sts.

Change to 4½mm (US size 7) needles.

Beg with a K row (chart row 1), work stripe chart patt in st st – between markers for chosen size – until chart row 31 (37: 37) has been completed and at the same time inc 1 st at each end of 6th (7th: 7th) row and then every foll 5th (6th: 6th)

row 5 times, ending with a RS row. 40 (44: 48) sts.

Cont stripe chart patt in st st throughout, work straight/even for 7 (5: 9) rows, ending with a WS row.

Cast/bind off 4 (5: 5) sts at beg of next 4 rows. 24 (24: 28) sts.

Cast/bind off 5 (5: 6) sts at beg of next 4 rows. Cast/bind off rem 4 sts.

SHOULDER BUTTON BAND

Using 4mm (US size 6) needles and yarn **C**, cast on 23 (25: 27) sts.

Beg with a K row, work 6 rows in st st, ending with a WS row.

K 2 rows.

Cast/bind off knitwise.

SHOULDER BUTTONHOLE BAND

Using 4mm (US size 6) needles and yarn **C**, cast on 23 (25: 27) sts.

Beg with a K row, work 4 rows in st st, ending with a WS row.

Next row (buttonhole row) (RS) K2 (3: 4), [yf, K2tog, K4] 3 times, yf, K2tog, K1 (2: 3).

P 1 row.

K 2 rows.

Cast/bind off knitwise.

NECK EDGING

Using 4mm (US size 6) needles and yarn **C**, cast on 60 (64: 68) sts.

Rib row 1 (RS) K1, *P2, K2, rep from * to last 3 sts, P2, K1.

Row 2 (WS) P1, *K2, P2, rep from * to last 3 sts, K2, P1.

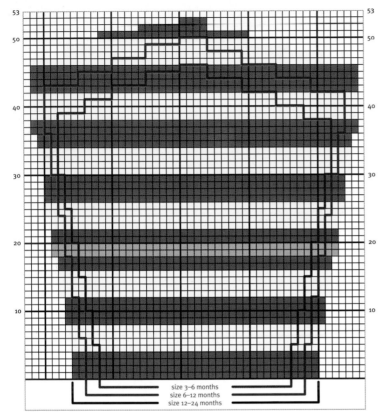

size 3–6 months
size 6–12 months
size 12–24 months

STRIPY SWEATER CHART SLEEVE

chart key

☐ **A**

■ **B**

■ **C**

Rep last 2 rows twice more.

Cast/bind off in rib.

TO FINISH

Press pieces lightly on WS following
instructions on yarn label and avoiding ribbing.

Weave in all loose ends.

Sew right shoulder seam.

Sew neck edging to neck edge of back and
front.

Sew button band to left front shoulder edge
and neck edging.

Sew buttonhole band to left back shoulder
edge and neck edging. Overlap buttonhole
band over button band and pin.

Fold top of each sleeve in half to find centre
and mark with a pin. Sew sleeves to armholes,
matching centre of top of sleeve to shoulder
seam or centre of buttonhole band.

Sew side and sleeve seams, carefully matching
stripe patt.

Sew buttons to button band to correspond
with buttonholes.

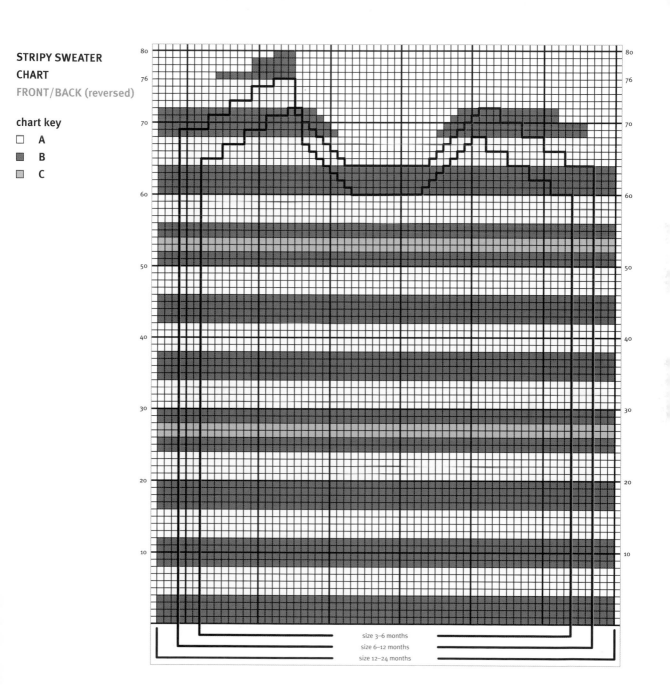

**STRIPY SWEATER
CHART**

FRONT/BACK (reversed)

chart key

☐ A

■ B

☐ C

size 3–6 months

size 6–12 months

size 12–24 months

BRIGHT AND SNUGGLY

girl's Fair Isle jacket

Show off your Fair Isle knitting skills and make this capacious comfy jacket for a girl who needs to keep warm and snug. Chunky yarn in subtle shades are a treat to knit with.

SIZES & MEASUREMENTS

To fit

2–3	3–4	4–5	years

Knitted measurements

Around chest

80	86	94	cm
31½	34	37	in

Length to shoulder

37	39	41	cm
14½	15¼	16	in

Sleeve seam

32	34	36	cm
12¾	13½	14½	in

YARN

Rowan Little Big Wool (50g/1¾oz per ball) as foll:

A pink/Garnet 503, 3 balls
B dark purple/Jasper 505, 2 balls
C pale pink/Onyx 501, 2 balls
D mid purple/Amethyst 504, 3 balls
E pale blue/Aquamarine 502, 2 balls
F white/Quartz 506, 2 balls

NEEDLES & EXTRAS

Pair of 7½mm (US size 10½) knitting needles
Pair of 8mm (US size 11) knitting needles
3 buttons

TENSION/GAUGE

11 sts and 15 rows to 10cm/4in measured over st st using 8mm (US size 11) needles.

ABBREVIATIONS

See page 9.

CHART NOTE

Work the chart pattern in stocking/stockinette stitch. Read all odd-numbered (knit) chart rows from right to left and all even-numbered (purl) chart rows from left to right. Use the Fair Isle technique for the chart pattern rows where two colours are used in a row, weaving colour not in use into wrong side of knitting.

BACK

Using 7½mm (US size 10½) needles and yarn **A**, cast on 45 (49: 53) sts.

Rib row 1 (RS) *K2, P2, rep from * to last st, K1.

Rib row 2 P1, *K2, P2, rep from * to end.

Rep last 2 rows once more.

Break off yarn **A**.

Change to 8mm (US size 11) needles.

Beg with a K row (chart row 1), work chart patt in st st – between markers for chosen size – until chart row 24 (25: 26) has been completed, ending with a WS (RS: WS) row.

Shape armholes

Cont in st st chart patt throughout, dec 1 st at each end of next row and then foll alt row. 41 (45: 49) sts.

Work straight/even until chart row 50 (52: 54) has been completed, ending with a WS row.

Shape right neck edge and shoulder

Next row (RS) K12 (13: 14), then turn, leaving rem 29 (32: 35) sts on a stitch holder.

Work on these 12 (13: 14) sts only for right side of neck.

Dec 1 st at beg of next row (neck edge) and cast/bind off last 5 (6: 6) sts of same row.

Rejoin yarn and cast/bind off rem 6 (6: 7) sts.

Shape left neck edge and shoulder

With RS facing, rejoin yarn to sts on holder and cast/bind off centre 17 (19: 21) sts, then K to end. 12 (13: 14) sts.

Next row (WS) Cast/bind off first 5 (6: 6) sts, P to last 2 sts, P2tog.

Cast/bind off rem 6 (6: 7) sts.

RIGHT FRONT

Using 7½mm (US size 10½) needles and yarn **A**, cast on 20 (22: 24) sts.

Rib row 1 (RS) K1 (2: 1), ^P2, K2, rep from * to last 3 (4: 3) sts, P2, K1 (2: 1).

Rib row 2 P1 (2: 1), *K2, P2, rep from * to last 3 (4: 3) sts, K2, P1 (2: 1). Rep last 2 rows once more.

Break off yarn **A**.

Change to 8mm (US size 11) needles.

Beg with a K row (chart row 1), work chart patt in st st – between markers for chosen size – until chart row 24 (25: 26) has been completed, ending with a WS (RS: WS) row.**

Shape armhole

Cont in st st chart patt throughout, dec 1 st at end (beg: end) of next row (armhole edge) and then at same edge on foll alt row, ending with a RS (WS: RS) row. 18 (20: 22) sts.

Shape neck

Dec 1 st at end (beg: end) of next row (neck edge) and then at same edge on every foll 3rd row 6 (7: 8) times, ending with a WS row. 11 (12: 13) sts.

Work straight/even until chart row 51 (53: 55) has been completed, ending with a RS row.

Cast/bind off 5 (6: 6) sts at beg of next row.

Cast/bind off rem 6 (6: 7) sts.

LEFT FRONT

Work as for right front to **.

Shape armhole

Cont in st st chart patt throughout, dec 1 st at beg (end: beg) of next row (armhole edge) and then at same edge on foll alt row, ending with a RS (WS: RS) row. 18 (20: 22) sts.

Shape neck

Dec 1 st at beg (end: beg) of next row (neck

edge) and then at same edge on every foll 3rd row 6 (7: 8) times, ending with a WS row. 11 (12: 13) sts.

Work straight/even until chart row 51 (53: 55) has been completed, ending with a RS row. Cast/bind off 5 (6: 6) sts at end of next row. Rejoin yarn and cast/bind off rem 6 (6: 7) sts.

SLEEVES (make 2)

Using 7½mm (US size 10½) needles and yarn **A**, cast on 24 (26: 30) sts.

Rib row 1 (RS) *K2, P2, rep from * to last 0 (2: 2) sts, K0 (2: 2).

Rib row 2 P0 (2: 2), *K2, P2, rep from * to end.

Rep last 2 rows 3 times more.

Break off yarn **A**.

Change to 8mm (US size 11) needles.

For 1st size only

Beg with a K row, work 1 row in yarn **F**.

For 2nd size only

Beg with a K row, work 2 rows in yarn **E** and 1 row in yarn **F**, inc 1 st at each end of last row. – (28: –) sts.

For 3rd size only

Beg with a K row, work 2 rows in yarn **C**, 2 rows in yarn **E** and 1 row in yarn **F**, inc 1 st at each end of last row. – (–: 32) sts.

For all sizes

Using yarn **D**, P 1 row. 24 (28: 32) sts.

Beg with a K row (chart row 1), work chart patt in st st – between markers for chosen size – until chart row 27 has been completed and at the same time inc 1 st at each end of 3rd row and then every foll 4th row 6 times, ending with a RS row. 38 (42: 46) sts.

Cont chart patt in st st throughout, work

straight/even for 3 (4: 5) rows, ending with a WS (RS: WS) row.

Shape top of sleeve

For 1st size only

Dec 1 st at each end of next row and then 2 foll alt rows. 32 (–: –) sts.

For 2nd size only

Dec 1 st at each end of next row and then foll alt row. – (38: –) sts.

For all sizes

Dec 1 st at each end of next 6 (9: 13) rows. 20 sts.

Cast/bind off rem 20 sts.

COLLAR AND BUTTON BAND

Using 7½mm (US size 10½) needles and yarn **A**, cast on 68 (74: 80) sts.

Break off yarn **A**.

Using yarn **D** for remainder of band, cont as foll:

Rib row 1 (RS) K1 (2: 1), *P2, K2, rep from * to last 3 (4: 3) sts, P2, K1 (2: 1).

Rib row 2 P1 (2: 1), *K2, P2, rep from * to last 3 (4: 3) sts, K2, P1 (2: 1).

Rep last 2 rows 3 times more, ending with a WS row.

Keeping rib correct as set throughout, cast/bind off 21 (22: 23) sts at beg of next row. 47 (52: 57) sts.

Dec 1 st at end of next row.

Dec 1 st at beg of next row.

Rep last 2 rows twice more. 41 (46: 51) sts.

Dec 1 st at end of next row. (A total of 16 rows have been completed from cast-on edge.)

Cast/bind off rem 40 (45: 50) sts in rib.

Rib row 4 (buttonhole row) (WS) Keeping rib correct as set, work first 4 sts in rib, [yrn, work 2 sts tog, work 6 sts in rib] twice, yrn, work 2 sts tog, work in rib to end.

Keeping rib correct as set throughout, work 2 rows more in rib, ending with a WS row.

Cast/ bind off 21 (22: 23) sts at end of next row. 47 (52: 57) sts.

Rejoin yarn and dec 1 st at beg of next row.

Dec 1 st at end of next row.

Rep last 2 rows twice more. 41 (46: 51) sts.

Dec 1 st at beg of next row. (A total of 16 rows have been completed from cast-on edge.)

Cast/bind off rem 40 (45: 50) sts in rib.

TO FINISH

Press pieces lightly on WS following instructions on yarn label and avoiding ribbing.

Weave in all loose ends.

Sew shoulder seams.

Sew together widest ends of collar/band pieces. Positioning back collar seam at centre of back neck and buttonhole band on right front, pin then sew cast/bound-off edge of collar/band to back and fronts.

Fold top of each sleeve in half to find centre and mark with a pin. Sew sleeves to armholes, matching centre of top of sleeve to shoulder seam and aligning Fair Isle patt.

Sew side and sleeve seams, matching Fair Isle patt.

Sew on buttons to correspond with buttonholes.

COLLAR AND BUTTONHOLE BAND

Using 7½mm (US size 10½) needles and yarn **A**, cast on 68 (74: 80) sts.

Break off yarn **A**.

Using yarn **D** for remainder of band, cont as foll:

Rib row 1 (RS) K1 (2: 1), *P2, K2, rep from * to last 3 (4: 3) sts, P2, K1 (2: 1).

Rib row 2 P1 (2: 1), *K2, P2, rep from * to last 3 (4: 3) sts, K2, P1 (2: 1).

Rib row 3 Rep row 1.

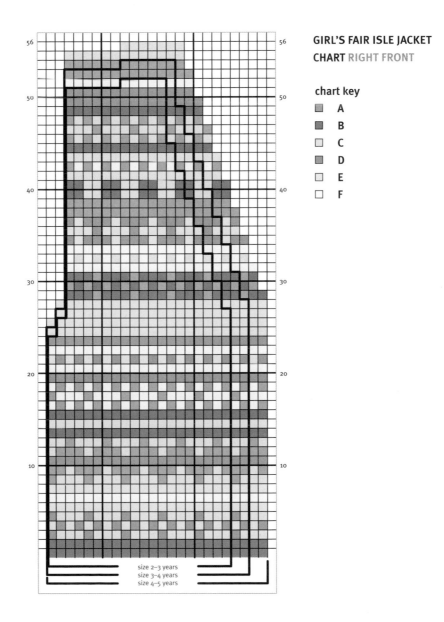

GIRL'S FAIR ISLE JACKET
CHART RIGHT FRONT

chart key
- A
- B
- C
- D
- E
- F

size 2–3 years
size 3–4 years
size 4–5 years

GIRL'S FAIR ISLE JACKET CHART BACK

chart key

- A
- B
- C
- D
- E
- F

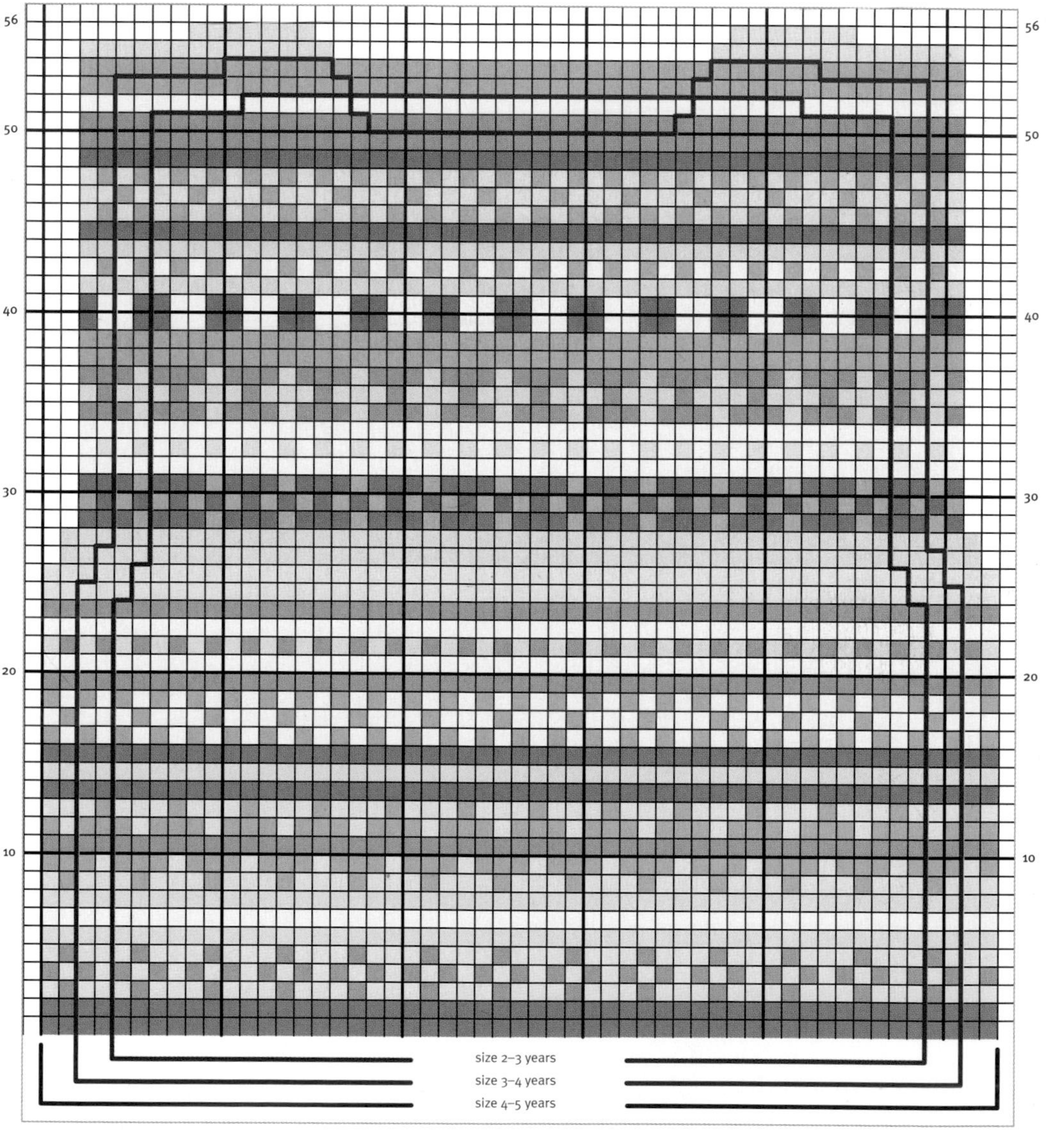
56
50
40
30
20
10
size 2–3 years
size 3–4 years
size 4–5 years

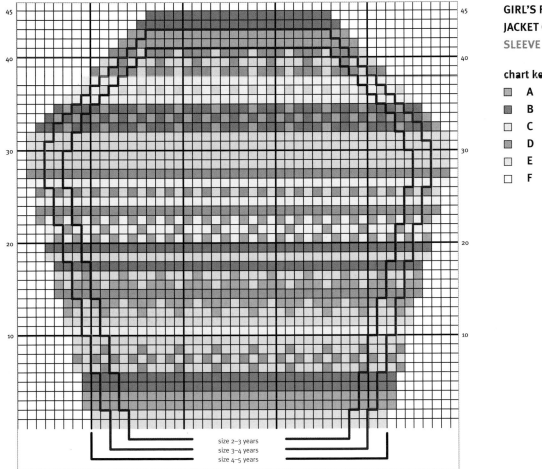

GIRL'S FAIR ISLE JACKET CHART

SLEEVE

chart key

A	
B	
C	
D	
E	
F	

size 2–3 years
size 3–4 years
size 4–5 years

Fair Isle hat and mittens

Knitted in a soft mohair-mix yarn, this girl's hat and mittens are a very stylish duo. The earflaps make the hat extra-warm, and the mittens' string means they'll never get lost.

SIZES

To fit

2–3	4–5	6–7	years

YARN

Hat

Rowan Kid Classic (50g/1³/₄oz per ball):

A red/Cherry Red 847, 1 ball

B pale pink/Sherbert Dip 850, 1 ball

C dark blue/Nighty 846, 1 ball

D plum/Victoria 852, 1 ball

E light green/Battle 845, 1 ball

F light brown/Bear 817, 1 ball

Mittens

Rowan Kid Classic (50g/1³/₄oz per ball):

A red/Cherry Red 847, 1 ball

B pale pink/Sherbert Dip 850, 1 ball

C dark blue/Nighty 846, 1 ball

D plum/Victoria 852, 1 ball

NOTE: If you are making both hat and mittens, one ball in each shade is enough for both.

NEEDLES

Hat

Pair of 5mm (US size 8) knitting needles

4mm (US size 6) circular knitting needle

Mittens

Pair of 4mm (US size 6) knitting needles

Pair of 5mm (US size 8) knitting needles

TENSION/GAUGE

18 sts and 24 rows to 10cm/4in measured over st st using 5mm (US size 8) needles.

ABBREVIATIONS

See page 9.

CHART NOTE

Work the chart patterns in stocking/stockinette stitch. Read all odd-numbered (knit) chart rows from right to left and all even-numbered (purl) chart rows from left to right. Use the Fair Isle technique for the chart pattern rows where two colours are used in a row, weaving colour not in use into wrong side of knitting.

HAT

Earflaps (make 2)

Earflaps are made first and then joined in when main section of hat is begun.

Using 5mm (US size 8) needles and yarn **B** (**B: E**), cast on 7 sts.

Beg with a K row, work 2 rows in st st, ending with a WS row.

Cont in st st throughout, work earflap for different sizes as foll:

For 3rd size only

Inc 1 st at each end of next row. – (–: 9) sts.
P 1 row.

For 2nd and 3rd sizes only

Break off yarn **B** for 2nd size.

Using yarn **E**, inc 1 st at each end of next row. – (9: 11) sts.

Using yarn **E**, P 1 row.

Break off yarn **E**.

For all sizes

Using yarn **D**, inc 1 st at each end of next row. 9 (11: 13) sts.

Using yarn **D**, P 1 row.

Break off yarn **D**.

Using yarn **F**, inc 1 st at each end of next row (this is chart row 1). 11 (13: 15) sts.

Break off yarn **F**.

Breaking off and joining in yarns as required and beg with a P row (chart row 2), work chart patt in st st – between markers for chosen size – until chart row 12 has been completed, ending with a WS row, *and at the same time* inc 1 st at each end of chart rows 3, 5 and 7.

Break off yarn **A** and leave these 17 (19: 21) sts on a stitch holder.

Make second earflap exactly as for first earflap.

Main section of hat

Using 5mm (US size 8) needles and using yarn **A**, cast on 12 (13: 14) sts onto right-hand needle and break off yarn; with WS of first earflap facing, slip these 17 (19: 21) sts onto right-hand needle; using yarn **A**, cast on 26 (28: 30) sts onto right-hand needle and break off yarn; with WS of second earflap facing, slip these 17 (19: 21) sts onto right-hand needle; using yarn **A**, cast on 12 (13: 14) sts onto right-hand needle and break off yarn. 84 (92: 100) sts.

Beg with a RS row, work next 10 rows in garter

st (K every row) in stripes as foll:

2 rows in yarn **B**, 2 rows in yarn **D**, 2 rows in yarn **E**, 2 rows in yarn **F** and 2 rows in yarn **C**, ending with a WS row.

Beg with a K row (chart row 1), work chart patt in st st – working 4-st rep 21 (23: 25) times – until chart row 12 has been completed, ending with a WS row.

Shape top of hat

Cont in st st, shape top of hat and work in stripes as foll:

Next row (RS) Using yarn **B**, K9 (10: 11), [dvdec, K18 (20: 22)] 3 times, dvdec, K9 (10: 11). 76 (84: 92) sts.

Using yarn **B**, K 1 row.

Using yarn **C** and beg with a K row, work 2 rows in garter st.

Next row (RS) Using yarn **E**, K8 (9: 10), [dvdec, K16 (18: 20)] 3 times, dvdec, K8 (9: 10). 68 (76: 84) sts.

Using yarn **E**, P 1 row.

Next row Using yarn **A**, K7 (8: 9), [dvdec, K14 (16: 18)] 3 times, dvdec, K7 (8: 9). 60 (68: 76) sts.

Using yarn **A**, P 1 row.

Next row Using yarn **B**, K6 (7: 8), [dvdec, K12 (14: 16)] 3 times, dvdec, K6 (7: 8). 52 (60: 68) sts.

Using yarn **B**, P 1 row.

Next row Using yarn **A**, K5 (6: 7), [dvdec, K10 (12: 14)] 3 times, dvdec, K5 (6: 7). 44 (52: 60) sts.

Using yarn **A**, K 1 row.

Next row Using yarn **B**, K4 (5: 6), [dvdec, K8 (10: 12)] 3 times, dvdec, K4 (5: 6). 36 (44: 52) sts.

Using yarn **B**, P 1 row.

Next row Using yarn **A**, K3 (4: 5), [dvdec, K6 (8: 10)] 3 times, dvdec, K3 (4: 5). 28 (36: 44) sts.

Using yarn **A**, P 1 row.

Next row Using yarn **B**, K2 (3: 4), [dvdec, K4 (6: 8)] 3 times, dvdec, K2 (3: 4). 20 (28: 36) sts.

Using yarn **B**, K 1 row.

Next row Using yarn **D**, K1 (2: 3), [dvdec, K2 (4: 6)] 3 times, dvdec, K1 (2: 3). 12 (20: 28) sts.

Using yarn **D**, P 1 row.

For 2nd and 3rd sizes only

Row 21 Using yarn **C**, K – (1: 2), [dvdec, K – (2: 4)] 3 times, dvdec, K – (1: 2). – (12: 20) sts.

Using yarn **C**, P 1 row.

For 3rd size only

Row 23 Using yarn **C**, K1, [dvdec, K2] 3 times, dvdec, K1. – (–: 12) sts.

Using yarn **C**, P 1 row.

For all sizes

Leaving rem 12 sts on needle, break off yarn, leaving a long tail-end to sew hat seam. Thread end of yarn onto a yarn needle and pass needle through remaining stitches while slipping them off knitting needle. Pull yarn to gather stitches and secure.

TO FINISH

Do NOT press.

Edging

With RS facing and using 4mm (US size 6) circular needles and yarn **A**, pick up and knit 11 (12: 13) sts along straight cast-on edge before earflap, 36 (40: 44) sts along edge of earflap, 24 (26: 28) sts along straight cast-on edge between earflaps, 36 (40: 44) sts along edge of

second earflap, and 11 (12: 13) sts along rem
straight cast-on edge. 118 (130: 142) sts.
Working back and forth in rows on circular
needle, K 1 row (a WS row).
Cast/bind off knitwise.
Using mattress stitch, sew hat seam, matching
stripes and Fair Isle patt.

Plait/braid for earflaps (make 2)

Cut six 1m/39in lengths each of yarns **A**, **B** and
D. Hold one group of six strands together and
fold in half. Then draw folded end through
stitch at centre of tip of one earflap, using a
crochet hook. Pull all 12 tail-ends of yarn
through loop at folded end and tighten firmly
to form a knot.
Attach two remaining groups of six strands in
same way, one at each side of first group.
Plait/braid three groups of strands to within
5cm/2in of end and knot together, leaving a
5cm/2in tassel at end.
Make another plait/braid on end of second
earflap in same way.

Pompom

Make a pompom, using strands of yarns **A**, **B**,
C, **D**, **E** and **F**. Then cut one 40cm/16in length
each of yarns **A**, **B** and **C**. Holding these 3
strands together, tie them tightly around
middle of pompom, positioning pompom at
centre of strands. Using 2 strands of each
yarn for each section of plait/braid, make a
plait/braid to ends of strands. Knot end and
sew to centre top of hat.

MITTENS

Main sections (make 2)

Using 4mm (US size 6) needles and yarn **A**,
cast on 30 (34: 38) sts.
Break off yarn **A**.
Using yarn **C**, work ribbing as foll:
Rib row 1 (RS) *K2, P2, rep from * to last 2 sts,
K2.
Rib row 2 *P2, K2, rep from * to last 2 sts, P2.
Rep last 2 rows 3 (4: 4) times more, ending
with a WS row.
Change to 5mm (US size 8) needles.
Breaking off and joining in yarns as required
and beg with a K row (chart row 1), work chart
patt in st st – between markers for chosen size
– until chart row 24 has been completed,
ending with a WS row.

Shape top of mitten

Cont in st st, shape top of mitten and work in
stripes as foll:
Next row (RS) Using yarn **D**, [K2, skp, K8 (10:
12), K2tog] twice, K2. 26 (30: 34) sts.
Using yarn **B**, P 1 row.
Next row Using yarn **B**, [K2, skp, K6 (8:10),
K2tog] twice, K2. 22 (26: 30) sts.

For 2nd and 3rd sizes only

Using yarn **D**, P 1 row.
Next row Using yarn **D**, [K2, skp, K – (6: 8),
K2tog] twice, K2. – (22: 26) sts.

For 3rd size only

Using yarn **A**, P 1 row.
Next row Using yarn **A**, [K2, skp, K6, K2tog]
twice, K2. – (–: 22) sts.

For all sizes

Next row Using yarn **D** (**A**: **A**), P2tog, P18,
P2tog.

Using yarn **D** (**A**: **A**), cast/bind off rem 20 sts.

Thumbs (make 2)

Using 5mm (US size 8) needles and yarn **C**,
cast on 4 sts.

Row 1 (RS) K to end.

Row 2 P to end.

Break off yarn **C**.

Shape thumb

Cont in st st in stripes, shape thumb as foll:

Row 3 Using yarn **B**, K into front and back of
first st, K to last st, K into front and back of last
st. 6 sts.

Row 4 Using yarn **B**, P to end.

Rows 5 and 6 Using yarn **A**, rep rows 3 and 4. 8
sts.

Rows 7 and 8 Using yarn **D**, rep rows 3 and 4.
10 sts.

Rows 9 and 10 Using yarn **C**, rep rows 3 and 4.
12 sts.

For 1st size only

Cont in st st throughout and working
straight/even, work 2 rows in yarn **B** and 2
rows in yarn **A**.

Using yarn **D**, dec 1 st at each end of each of
next 2 rows. 8 sts.

For 2nd size only

Cont in st st throughout and working
straight/even, work 2 rows in yarn **B**, 2 rows in
yarn **A** and 2 rows in yarn **D**.

Using yarn **C**, dec 1 st at each end of each of
next 2 rows. 8 sts.

For 3rd size only

Cont in st st throughout and using yarn **B**, inc 1
st at each end of next row. 14 sts.

Working straight/even, work 1 row in yarn **B**, 2

rows in yarn **A**, 2 rows yarn **D** and 2 rows in yarn **C**.

Using yarn **B**, dec 1 st at each end of each of next 2 rows. 10 sts.

For all sizes

Leaving rem 8 (8: 10) sts on needle, break off yarn, leaving a long tail-end to sew thumb seam. Thread end of yarn onto a yarn needle and pass needle through remaining stitches while slipping them off knitting needle. Pull yarn to gather stitches and secure.

TO FINISH

Fold thumbs in half and sew thumb seam at top of thumb, matching stripes and leaving first 8 (8: 10) rows from cast-on edge free for sewing to main section.

Sew a thumb to each mitten, aligning lower tip of thumb with chart row 5.

Sew side seams of mitten above and below thumb, matching the Fair Isle patt and stripes.

Using 2 strands each of yarns **A**, **B** and **C**, make a plait/braid about 1m/39in long and sew one end to each mitten. (This string needs to be long enough to pass through coat/jacket sleeves and hang out of each sleeve ready to be put on or left hanging when not in use.)

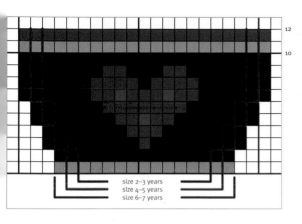

size 2–3 years
size 4–5 years
size 6–7 years

FAIR ISLE HAT CHART

EARFLAPS

chart key

- ■ A
- ■ C
- ■ D
- ■ E

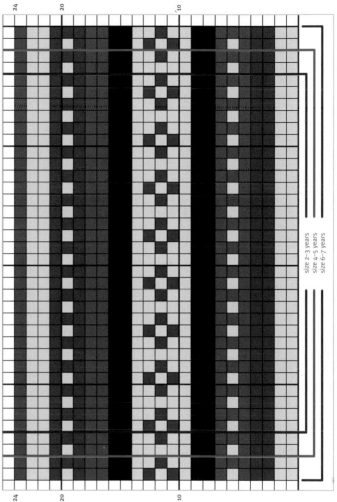

size 2–3 years
size 4–5 years
size 6–7 years

FAIR ISLE MITTENS

CHART MITTENS

chart key

- ■ A
- ☐ B
- ■ C
- ■ D

chunky Fair Isle sweater and scarf

The combination of a chunky wool yarn and a simple Fair Isle pattern makes this sweater a modern classic for boys and girls. Make the cosy matching scarf for a superwarm accessory.

SIZES & MEASUREMENTS

Sweater to fit

2–3	3–4	4–5	years

Knitted measurements

Around chest

70	75	80	cm
27$\frac{1}{2}$	29$\frac{1}{2}$	31$\frac{1}{2}$	in

Length to shoulder

38	41	44	cm
15	16	17$\frac{1}{4}$	in

Sleeve seam

31	32	34	cm
12$\frac{1}{4}$	12$\frac{3}{4}$	13$\frac{1}{4}$	in

Scarf

Finished scarf measures approximately 17cm/6$\frac{3}{4}$in wide by 115cm/45$\frac{1}{4}$in long.

YARN

Sweater

Rowan Big Wool (100g/3$\frac{1}{2}$oz per ball):

A off white/Sugar Spun 016, 3 balls

B pale blue/Ice Blue 021, 2 balls

C brown/ Camouflage 023, 1 ball

D red/Bohemian 028, 1 ball

Scarf

Rowan Big Wool (100g/3$\frac{1}{2}$oz per ball):

A off white/ Sugar Spun 016, 3 balls

B pale blue/Ice Blue 021, 1 ball

C brown/Camouflage 023, 1 ball

D red/Bohemian 028, 1 ball

E pale green/Pistachio 029, 1 ball

NEEDLES

Sweater

Pair of 12mm (US size 17) knitting needles
Pair of 10mm (US size 15) knitting needles

Scarf

Pair of 12mm (US size 17) knitting needles

TENSION/GAUGE

8 sts and 11 rows to 10cm/4in measured over
st st using 12mm (US size 17) knitting needles.

ABBREVIATIONS

See page 9.

CHART NOTE

Work the sweater chart pattern in stocking/
stockinette stitch. Read all odd-numbered
(knit) chart rows from right to left and all even-
numbered (purl) chart rows from left to right.
Work the scarf chart pattern in the same way,
but work specified rows in reverse stocking/
stockinette stitch.

Use the Fair Isle technique for the chart
pattern rows where two colours are used in a
row, weaving colour not in use into wrong side
of knitting.

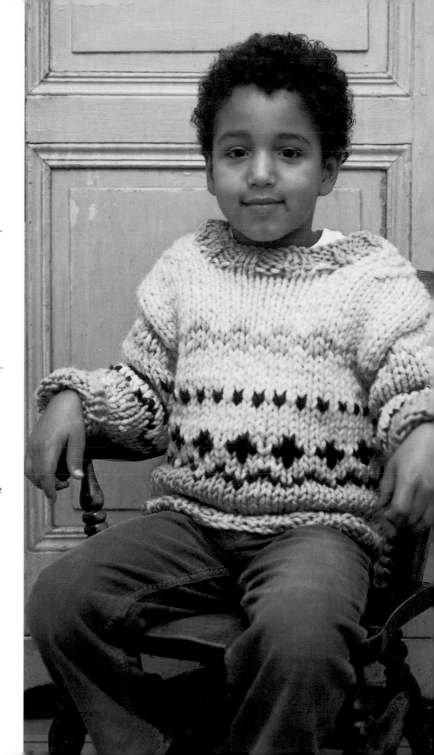

SWEATER

Back

Using 10mm (US size 15) needles and yarn **B**, cast on 28 (30: 32) sts.

Rib row 1 (RS) K1 (2: 1), *P2, K2, rep to last 3 (4: 3) sts, P2, K1 (2: 1).

Rib row 2 P1 (2: 1), *K2, P2, rep from * to last 3 (4: 3) sts, K2, P1 (2: 1).

Rep last 2 rows once more.

Change to 12mm (US size 17) needles.

Beg with a K row (chart row 1), work chart patt in st st – between markers for chosen size – until chart row 17 (20: 23) has been completed, ending with a RS (WS: RS) row.

Shape armholes

Working in chart patt, dec 1 st at each end of next row.

Work straight/even in chart patt until chart row 28 has been completed, ending with a WS row.

This completes Fair Isle patt.**

Cont is st st and yarn **A** only and beg with a K row, work straight/even for 7 (10:13) rows, ending with a RS (WS: RS) row.

Shape neck and shoulders

Shape neck and shoulders as foll:

For 1st and 3rd sizes only

Next row (WS) P8, then turn, leaving rem sts on a stitch holder.

Work on these 8 sts only for left side of neck.

Dec 1 st at beg of next row (neck edge). 7 sts.

Cast/bind off 3 sts at beg of next row.

Cast/bind off rem 4 sts.

With **WS** facing, rejoin yarn to sts on holder and cast/bind off centre 10 (–: 14) sts, then P to end. 8 sts.

Dec 1 st at end of next row (neck edge). 7 sts.

Cast/bind off 3 sts at end of next row.

Rejoin yarn and cast/bind off rem 4 sts.

For 2nd size only

Next row (RS) K8, then turn, leaving rem sts on a stitch holder.

Work on these 8 sts only for right side of neck.

Dec 1 st at beg of next row (neck edge). 7 sts.

Cast/bind off 3 sts at beg of next row.

Cast/bind off rem 4 sts.

With RS facing, rejoin yarn to sts on holder and cast/bind off centre 12 sts, then K to end. 8 sts.

Dec 1 st at end of next row (neck edge). 7 sts.

Cast/bind off 3 sts at end of next row.

Rejoin yarn and cast/bind off rem 4 sts.

Front

Work as for back to **.

Cont is st st and yarn **A** only and beg with a K row, work straight/even for 4 (7:10) rows, ending with a WS (RS: WS) row.

Shape neck and shoulders

Shape neck and shoulders as foll:

For 1st and 3rd sizes only

Next row (RS) K9, then turn, leaving rem sts on a stitch holder.

Work on these 9 sts only for left side of neck.

Dec 1 st at beg of next row (neck edge). 8 sts.

Dec 1 st at end of next row (neck edge). 7 sts.

Beg with a P row, work straight/even for 2 rows.

Cast/bind off 3 sts at end of next row.

Rejoin yarn and cast/bind off rem 4 sts.

With RS facing, rejoin yarn to sts on holder and cast/bind off centre 8 (–: 12) sts, then K to end. 9 sts.

Dec 1 st at end of next row (neck edge). 8 sts.

Dec 1 st at beg of next row (neck edge). 7 sts.

Beg with a P row, work straight/even for 2 rows.

Cast/bind off 3 sts at beg of next row.

Cast/bind off rem 4 sts.

For 2nd size only

Next row (WS) P9, then turn, leaving rem sts on a stitch holder.

Work on these 9 sts only for right side of neck.

Dec 1 st at beg of next row (neck edge). 8 sts.

Dec 1 st at end of next row (neck edge). 7 sts.

Beg with a K row, work straight/even for 2 rows.

Cast/bind off 3 sts at end of next row.

Rejoin yarn and cast/bind off rem 4 sts.

With **WS** facing, rejoin yarn to sts on holder and cast/bind off centre 10 sts, then P to end. 9 sts.

Dec 1 st at end of next row (neck edge). 8 sts.

Dec 1 st at beg of next row (neck edge). 7 sts.

Beg with a K row, work straight/even for 2 rows.

Cast/bind off 3 sts at beg of next row.

Cast/bind off rem 4 sts.

Sleeves (make 2)

Using 10mm (US size 15) needles and yarn **B**, cast on 14 (16: 18) sts.

Rib row 1 K2 (1: 2), *P2, K2, rep from * to last 4 (3: 4) sts, P2, K2 (1: 2).

Row 2 P2 (1: 2), *K2, P2, rep from * to last 4 (3: 4) sts, K2, P2 (1: 2).

Rep last 2 rows once more.

Change to 12mm (US size 17) needles.

Beg with a P (K: K) row, work 1 (2: 4) rows in st st and at the same time inc 1 st at each end of first (2nd: 3rd) of these rows. 16 (18: 20) sts.

Beg with a K row (chart row 1), work chart patt in st st – between markers for chosen size – until chart row 19 has been completed and at the same time inc 1 st at each end of 3rd row and then every foll 4th row 4 (4: 3) times, ending with a RS row. 26 (28: 28) sts.

Beg with a P row, work straight/even in chart patt for 3 rows.

Shape top of sleeve

Cont in chart patt throughout, dec 1 st at each end of next 6 (7: 7) rows.

Cast/bind off rem 14 sts.

Neck edging

Using 10mm (US size 15) needles and yarn **B**, cast on 38 (42: 46) sts.

Rib row 1 (RS) *K2, P2, rep from * to last 2 sts, K2.

Rib row 2 *P2, K2, rep from * to last 2 sts, P2.

Rep last 2 rows twice more.

Cast/bind off in rib.

TO FINISH

Press pieces lightly on WS following instructions on yarn label and avoiding ribbing.

Weave in all loose ends.

Sew right shoulder seam.

Pin, then sew neck edging to neck edge of

back and front.

Sew left shoulder seam and neck edging seam.

Fold top of each sleeve in half to find centre and mark with a pin. Sew sleeves to armholes, matching centre of top of sleeve to shoulder seam.

Sew side and sleeve seams, carefully matching Fair Isle patt.

SCARF

To make scarf

Scarf is worked in one long strip, then folded in half lengthwise and stitched tog along one long side.

Work 2 shaped ends for scarf before beginning main section as foll:

First shaped end

***Using 12mm (US size 17) needles and yarn **C**, cast on 4 sts.

Row 1 (RS) K to end.

Row 2 P into front and back of first st, P to last st, P into front and back of last st. 6 sts.

Row 3 K into front and back of first st, K to last st, K into front and back of last st. 8 sts.

Row 4 P to end.

Rows 5 and 6 Rep rows 3 and 4. 10 sts.

Rows 7 and 8 Rep rows 1 and 2. 12 sts.

Row 9 Rep row 1.***

Break off yarn **C** and slip these 12 sts onto a spare needle.

Second shaped end

Work as for first shaped end from *** to ***. 12 sts.

Row 10 (WS) P into front and back of first st,

P10, P into front and back of next st, then with WS facing, P into front and back of first st of first shaped end on spare needle, P10, P into front and back of last st. 28 sts.

Begin Fair Isle pattern

Beg with a K row (chart row 1), work chart patt in st st until chart row 3 has been completed, ending with a RS row.

Work next 2 rows in rev st st, by knitting chart row 4 (WS) and purling chart row 5 (RS).

Beg with a P row, work chart rows 6–18 in st st.

Work next 2 rows in rev st st, by purling chart row 19 (RS) and knitting chart row 20 (WS).

Beg with a K row, work chart rows 21–48 in st st.

Work next 2 rows in rev st st, by purling chart row 49 (RS) and knitting chart row 50 (WS).

Beg with a K row, work chart rows 51–58 in st st.

Work next 2 rows in rev st st, by purling chart row 59 (RS) and knitting chart row 60 (WS).

Beg with a K row, work chart rows 61–88 in st st.

Work next 2 rows in rev st st, by purling chart row 89 (RS) and knitting chart row 90 (WS).

Beg with a K row, work chart rows 91–103 in st st.

Work next 2 rows in rev st st, by knitting chart row 104 (WS) and purling chart row 105 (RS).

Beg with a P row, work rows 106–108 in st st, ending with a WS row.

Shape ends

Cont with yarn **C** only.

Next row (RS) K2tog, K10, K2tog, then turn,

leaving rem 14 sts on a stitch holder.

Work first shaped end on these 12 sts as foll:

****Beg with a P row, work straight/even in st st for 2 rows in st st.

Next row P2tog, P to last 2 sts, P2tog. 10 sts.

Beg with a K row, work straight in st st for 2 rows.

Next row K2tog, K to last 2 sts, K2tog. 8 sts.

P 1 row.

Next row K2tog, K to last 2 sts, K2tog. 6 sts.

Next row P2tog, P to last 2 sts, P2tog.

Cast/bind off rem 4 sts.****

With RS facing, rejoin yarn **C** to sts on holder, K2tog, K to last 2 sts, K2tog.

Work as for first shaped end from **** to ****.

TO FINISH

Fold scarf in half lengthwise and sew centre seam and end seams, carefully matching Fair Isle patt.

Embroidery

Using a blunt-ended yarn needle and yarn **B**, sew around ends of scarf in blanket stitch.

Pompoms and plaits/braids

Make 2 large pompoms using a mixture of yarns **A**, **B**, **C**, **D** and **E**.

Then make 2 plaits/braids 10–14cm/4–5$\frac{1}{2}$in long using 4 strands of yarn **B** for each of three sections of each plait/braid. Sew one plait/braid to each end of scarf, leaving one long end of yarn at end of plait/braid to tie on pompoms. Tie a p
ompom to end of each plait/braid making a firm knot.

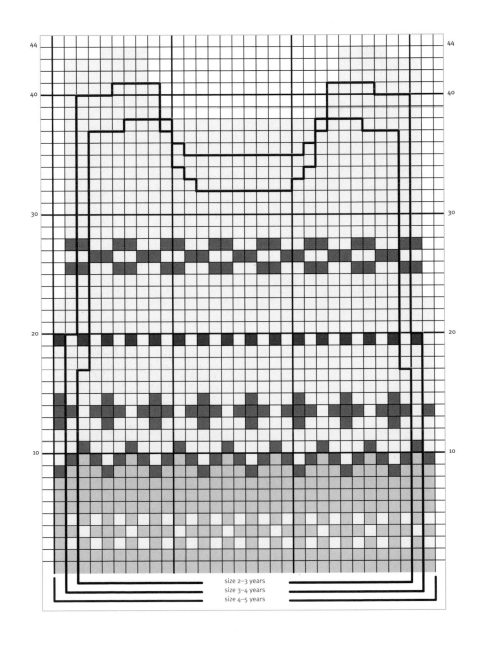

**CHUNKY FAIR
ISLE SWEATER
CHART**

FRONT/BACK
(reversed)

chart key

☐	A
▨	B
▨	C
■	D

size 2–3 years
size 3–4 years
size 4–5 years

chart key

A

B

C

D

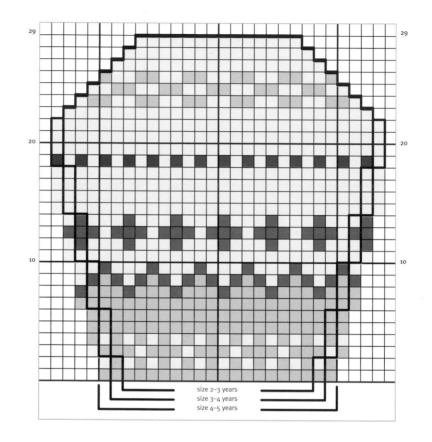

size 2–3 years
size 3–4 years
size 4–5 years

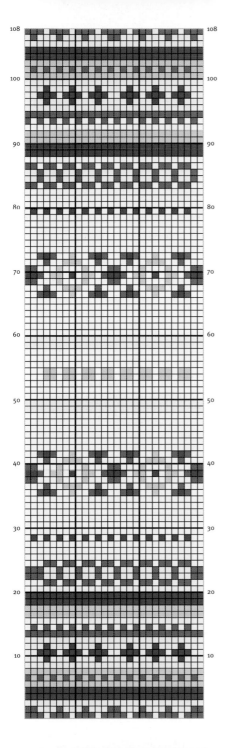

CHUNKY FAIR ISLE SCARF CHART

chart key

- ☐ A
- ☐ B
- ■ C
- ■ D
- ☐ E

pompom hat

Heigh, ho! Put on your hat before you go sledging down hills covered in snow. Worked in soft merino wool and bright hues, this hat will keep ears warm on frosty winter days.

SIZES

To fit

2–3   4–5   6–7   years

YARN

Jaeger Extra Fine Merino DK (50g/1¾oz per ball) as foll:

A red/Raspberry 943, 1 ball
B dark blue/Indigo 952, 1 ball
C light blue/Lagoon 997, 1 ball
D white/White 930, 1 ball

NEEDLES

Pair of 3¾mm (US size 5) knitting needles
Pair of 4mm (US size 6) knitting needles

TENSION/GAUGE

22 sts and 31 rows to 10cm/4in measured over st st using 4mm (US size 6) needles.

ABBREVIATIONS

See page 9.

CHART NOTE

Work the chart pattern in stocking/ stockinette stitch. Read all odd-numbered (knit) chart rows from right to left and all even-numbered (purl) chart rows from left to right.
Use the Fair Isle technique for the chart pattern rows where two colours are used in a row, weaving colour not in use into wrong side of knitting.

TO MAKE HAT

Using 3³⁄₄mm (US size 5) needles and yarn **A**, cast on 94 (98: 102) sts.

Rib row 1 (WS) *K2, P2, rep from * to last 2 sts, K2.

Rib row 2 *P2, K2, rep from * to last 2 sts, P2.

Rep last 2 rows 9 times more, then rep rib row 1 once more, ending with a WS row.

Change to 4mm (US size 6) needles.

Work chart pattern

Breaking off and joining in yarns as required, work stripe and Fair Isle chart patt as foll:

Beg with a K row (chart row 1), work chart patt in st st, working edge st then 4-st rep 23 (24: 25) times followed by edge st, until chart row 28 has been completed, ending with a WS row.

Shape top of hat

Cont in st st throughout, shape top of hat over next 12 rows of stripes as foll:

Shaping row 1 (RS) Using yarn **B**, K11 (11: 12), [K3tog, K20 (21: 22)] 3 times, K3tog, K11 (12: 12). 86 (90: 94) sts.

Shaping row 2 Using yarn **D**, P10 (11: 11), [P3tog, P18 (19: 20)] 3 times, P3tog, P10 (10: 11). 78 (82: 86) sts.

Shaping row 3 Using yarn **D**, K9 (9: 10), [K3tog, K16 (17: 18)] 3 times, K3tog, K9 (10: 10). 70 (74: 78) sts.

Shaping row 4 Using yarn **A**, P8 (9: 9), [P3tog, P14 (15: 16)] 3 times, P3tog, P8 (8: 9). 62 (66: 70) sts.

Shaping row 5 Using yarn **A**, K7 (7: 8), [K3tog, K12 (13: 14)] 3 times, K3tog, K7 (8: 8). 54 (58: 62) sts.

Shaping row 6 Using yarn **C**, P6 (7: 7), [P3tog,

P10 (11: 12)] 3 times, P3tog, P6 (6: 7). 46 (50: 54) sts.

Shaping row 7 Using yarn **C**, K5 (5: 6), [K3tog, K8 (9: 10)] 3 times, K3tog, K5 (6: 6). 38 (42: 46) sts.

Shaping row 8 Using yarn **B**, P4 (5: 5), [P3tog, P6 (7: 8)] 3 times, P3tog, P4 (4: 5). 30 (34: 38) sts.

Shaping row 9 Using yarn **B**, K3 (3: 4), [K3tog, K4 (5: 6)] 3 times, K3tog, K3 (4: 4). 22 (26: 30) sts.

Shaping row 10 Using yarn **D**, P2 (3: 3), [P3tog, P2 (3: 4)] 3 times, P3tog, P2 (2: 3). 14 (18: 22) sts.

Shaping row 11 Using yarn **D**, K1 (1: 2), [K3tog, K0 (1: 2)] 3 times, K3tog, K1 (2: 2). 6 (10: 14) sts.

Shaping row 12 Using yarn **D**, P1, [P3tog] 1 (3: 4) times, P2 (0: 1).

Leaving rem 4 (4: 6) sts on needle, break off yarn, leaving a long tail-end to sew hat seam.

TO FINISH

Thread end of yarn onto a blunt-ended yarn needle and pass needle through remaining stitches while slipping them off knitting needle. Pull yarn to gather stitches and secure. Using mattress stitch, sew hat seam to ribbing, then turn hat inside out and sew ribbing seam with wrong side of hat facing. Using yarn **B**, make a pompom and sew to top of hat.

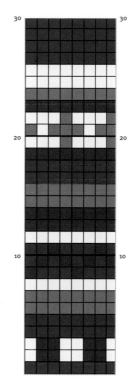

POMPOM HAT CHART

chart key
- ■ **A**
- ■ **B**
- ■ **C**
- □ **D**

PICTURE PERFECT

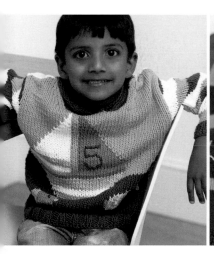

heart sweater

With a simple heart motif on the front and back, this wool and cotton sweater can be dressed up or down to suit any occasion. For an the extra-special finish, embroider flowers on the hearts.

SIZES & MEASUREMENTS

To fit

3–4	4–5	5–6	6–7	years

Knitted measurements

Around chest

72	76	80	84	cm
$28^1/_4$	30	$31^1/_2$	33	in

Length to shoulder

40	42	44	46	cm
$15^3/_4$	$16^1/_2$	$17^1/_4$	18	in

Sleeve seam

31	33	35	37	cm
$12^1/_4$	13	$13^3/_4$	$14^1/_2$	in

YARN

Sweater

6 (6: 6:7) 50g/$1^3/_4$oz balls of Rowan Wool
Cotton in **A** (pale pink/Tender 951)
One 50g/$1^3/_4$oz ball of Rowan Wool
Cotton in **B** (dark pink/Rich 911)

Embroidery

Use leftover yarns for embroidery **or** purchase
one ball each of Rowan Wool Cotton in
C (burgundy/Gypsy 910), **D** (pale purple/Violet
933), **E** (pale blue/ Clear 941) and **F** (dull
green/Riviera 930)

NEEDLES

Pair of $3^3/_4$mm (US size 5) knitting needles
Pair of 4mm (US size 6) knitting needles

TENSION/GAUGE

23 sts and 31 rows to 10cm/4in measured over
st st using 4mm (US size 6) needles.

ABBREVIATIONS

See page 9.

CHART NOTE

Work the chart motifs in stocking/
stockinette stitch. Read all odd-numbered
(knit) chart rows from right to left and all
even-numbered (purl) chart rows from left to
right. Use the intarsia technique for the chart
motifs, using a separate length of yarn for
each area of colour and twisting the yarns
together on the wrong side of the work
where they meet.

BACK

Using 3¾mm (US size 5) needles and yarn B, cast on 84 (88: 92: 96) sts.

Rib row 1 (RS) Using yarn **B**, *K2, P2, rep from * to end.

Break off yarn **B**.

Continue with yarn **A** only, rep last row 19 times more, ending with a WS row.**

Change to 4mm (US size 6) needles.

Beg with a K row, work 46 (48: 52: 56) rows in st st, ending with a WS row.

Shape armholes

Beg with a K row and cont in st st throughout, dec 1 st at each end of next row and then 2 foll alt rows, ending with RS row. 78 (82: 86: 90) sts.

Work straight/even for 15 rows.

Position heart motif

Using chart for Heart 1, position chart motif on next 2 rows as foll:

Next row (RS) K32 (34: 36: 38), work 15 sts from chart row 1 for Heart 1, K31 (33: 35: 37).

Next row P31 (33: 35: 37), work 15 sts from chart row 2 for Heart 1, P32 (34: 36: 38).

Cont heart motif as set, work straight/even until all 16 rows of chart have been completed, ending with a WS row.

Break off yarn **B** and cont with yarn **A** only.

Work straight/even for 16 (20: 22: 24) rows, ending with a WS row.

Shape shoulders

Beg shoulder shaping as foll:

Cast/bind off 3 (3: 4: 5) sts at beg of next 2 rows.

Next row (RS) Cast/bind off first 3 (4: 4: 4) sts, K until there are 26 sts on right-hand needle, then turn, leaving rem sts 43 (46: 48: 50) sts on a stitch holder.

Work on these 26 sts only for right side of neck.

Shape right neck edge and shoulder

Dec 1 st at beg of next row (neck edge). 25 sts.

Next row (RS) Cast/bind off first 4 sts, K to last 2 sts, K2tog. 20 sts.

Cast/bind off 3 sts at beg of next row.

Next row (RS) Cast/bind off first 4 sts, K to last 2 sts, K2tog.

Rep last 2 rows once more. 4 sts.

P 1 row.

Cast/bind off.

Shape left neck edge and shoulder

With RS facing, rejoin yarn to sts on holder and cast/bind off centre 14 (16: 18: 20) sts, then K to end.

Next row (WS) Cast/bind off first 3 (4: 4: 4) sts, P to last 2 sts, P2tog. 25 sts.

Next row Cast/bind off 3 sts, knit to end.

Next row Cast/bind off first 4 sts, P to last 2 sts, P2tog.

Rep last 2 rows once more. 9 sts.

Dec 1 st at beg of next row (neck edge). 8 sts.

Cast/bind off 4 sts at beg of next row.
Cast/bind off rem 4 sts.

FRONT

Work as for back to **.
Change to 4mm (US size 6) needles.
Beg with a K row, work 36 (38: 42: 46) rows in st st, ending with a WS row.

Position heart motif
Using chart for Heart 2, position chart motif on next 2 rows as foll:
Next row (RS) K24 (26: 28: 30), work 37 sts from chart row 1 for Heart 2, K23 (25: 27: 29).
Next row P23 (25: 27: 29), work 37 sts from chart row 2 for Heart 2, P24 (26: 28: 30).
Cont heart motif as set and working in st st throughout, work straight/even until first 10 chart have been completed, ending with a WS row.

Shape armholes
Cont heart motif as set, dec 1 st at each end of next row and then 2 foll alt rows, ending with RS row. 78 (82: 86: 90) sts.
Cont heart motif as set, work straight/even until chart row 36 has been completed, ending with a WS row.
Break off yarn **B** and cont with yarn **A** only.
Work straight/even for 20 (24: 26: 28) rows, ending with a WS row.

Shape left neck edge and shoulder
Next row (RS) K27 (28: 29: 30), then turn, leaving rem 51 (54: 57: 60) sts on a stitch holder.
Work on these 27 (28: 29: 30) sts only for left side of neck.
Dec 1 st at beg of next row (neck edge) and

then at beg of 2 foll alt rows, ending with a WS row. 24 (25: 26: 27) sts.
Cast/bind off 3 (3: 4: 5) sts at beg of next row (shoulder edge). 21 (22: 22: 22) sts.
Dec 1 st at beg of next row. 20 (21: 21: 21) sts.
Cast/bind off 3 (4: 4: 4) sts at beg of next row. 17 sts.
Dec 1 st at beg of next row. 16 sts.
Cast/bind off 4 sts at the beg of next row.
P 1 row.
Rep last 2 rows twice more.
Cast/bind off rem 4 sts.

Shape right neck edge and shoulder
With RS facing, rejoin yarn to sts on holder and cast/bind off centre 24 (26: 28: 30) sts, then K to end. 27 (28: 29: 30) sts.
Dec 1 st at end of next row (neck edge) and then at end of 2 foll alt rows, ending with a WS row. 24 (25: 26: 27) sts.
K 1 row.
Next row (WS) Cast/bind off first 3 (3: 4: 5) sts, P to last 2 sts, P2tog. 20 (21: 21: 21) sts.
K 1 row.
Next row Cast/bind off first 3 (4: 4: 4) sts, P to last 2 sts, P2tog. 16 sts.
K 1 row.
Cast/bind off 4 sts at beg of next row.
Rep last 2 rows twice more.
Cast/bind off rem 4 sts.

SLEEVES (make 2)

Using 3¾mm (US size 5) needles and yarn **B**, cast on 40 (44: 48: 52) sts.
Rib row 1 (RS) Using yarn **B**, *K2, P2, rep from * to end.
Break off yarn **B**.

Cont with yarn **A** only, rep last row 19 times more, ending with a WS row.

Change to 4mm (US size 6) needles.

Beg with a K row, work 2 rows in st st.

Cont in st st throughout, inc 1 st at each end of next row and then every foll 4th row 12 (13: 14: 15) times, ending with a RS row. 66 (72: 78: 84) sts.

Work straight/even for 13 rows, ending with a WS row.

Shape top of sleeve

Dec 1 st at each end of next row and then 2 foll alt rows, ending with a RS row.

P 1 row.

Cast/bind off 5 sts at beg of every row until 10 (6: 12: 8) sts rem.

Cast/bind off.

NECK EDGING

Using 3³⁄₄mm (US size 5) needles and yarn **B**, cast on 82 (90: 98: 106) sts.

Rib row 1 (RS) Using yarn **B**, *K2, P2, rep from * to last 2 sts, K2.

Break off yarn **B**.

Rib row 2 Using yarn **A**, *P2, K2, rep from * to last 2 sts, P2.

Using yarn **A** only, rep last 2 rows 3 times more.

Cast/bind off in rib.

TO FINISH

Press pieces lightly on WS following instructions on yarn label and avoiding ribbing.

Sew left shoulder seam. Pin then sew neck edging to neck edge.

Sew right shoulder seam and neck edging seam.

Fold top of each sleeve in half to find centre and mark with a pin. Sew sleeves to armholes, matching centre of top of sleeve to shoulder seam.

Sew side and sleeve seams.

EMBROIDERY

Work embroidery using a blunt-ended yarn needle and lazy daisy stitch, straight stitch, backstitch or French knots.

HEART SWEATER CHART FRONT

chart key
☐ A
■ B

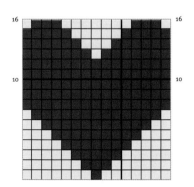

HEART SWEATER CHART BACK

chart key
☐ A
■ B

fairyland blanket

Knitted using the intarsia technique, this gorgeous fairyland scene would light up any baby's bedroom. The simple embroidered details provide the perfect finishing touches.

SIZE

Finished blanket measures approximately 95cm/37½in by 115cm/45¼in, including edging.

YARN

Jaeger Matchmaker Merino DK (50g/1¾oz per ball) as foll:

A light green/Sage 857, 2 balls
B pale baby blue/Feather 864, 1 ball
C pale pink/Petal 883, 2 balls
D mid purple/Parma 888, 2 balls
E dusty pink/Rosy 870, 1 ball
F dusty purple/Geranium 894, 2 balls
G bright pink/Rock Rose 896, 2 balls
H dark teal/Teal 790, 1 ball
J dark purple/Azalea 897, 1 ball
L light yellow-green/Hop 899, 2 balls
M blue-green/Marine 914, 2 balls
N pale grey-blue/Putty 892, 2 balls

NEEDLES

Pair of 4mm (US size 6) knitting needles

TENSION/GAUGE

22 sts and 30 rows to 10cm/4in measured over st st chart patt using 4mm (US size 6) needles.

ABBREVIATIONS

See page 9.

CHART NOTE

Work the chart pattern in stocking/stockinette stitch. Read all odd-numbered (knit) chart rows from right to left and all even-numbered (purl) chart rows from left to right. Use the intarsia technique for the chart pattern, using a separate length of yarn for each area of colour and twisting the yarns together on the wrong side of the work where they meet.

TO MAKE BLANKET

Using 4mm (US size 6) needles and yarn **A**, cast on 183 sts.

Beg with a K row (chart row 1), work chart patt in st st until chart row 320 has been completed, ending with a WS row. Cast/bind off.

EDGING STRIPS (make 4)

Using 4mm (US size 6) needles and yarn **G**, cast on 2 sts.

Work first edging strip in garter st (K every row) as foll:

Row 1 (WS) K to end.

Row 2 (inc row) (RS) K into front and back of first st, K to end. 3 sts.

Rows 3–16 Rep rows 1 and 2 seven times. 10 sts.

Mark beg of last row with a contrasting yarn.

Work straight/even in garter st until strip between marker and needle fits across top edge of blanket, ending with a WS row.

Shape other end of strip on same edge as first end as foll:

Next row (dec row) (RS) K2tog, K to end. 9 sts.

Next row K to end.

Rep last 2 rows 6 times, ending with a WS row. 3 sts.

Next row (dec row) (RS) K2tog, K1.

Cast/bind off rem 2 sts knitwise.

Work edging strips for other three sides of blanket in same way, but using yarn **F** for bottom strip, yarn **C** for left side edge, and yarn **D** for right side edge.

TO FINISH

Press blanket lightly on WS following instructions on yarn label. Do NOT press edging strips.

Pin each edging strip (between increase and decrease rows) to edge of blanket and sew in place.

Sew together diagonal ends of edging strips at corners of blanket.

Work embroidery next.

EMBROIDERY

Starting at lower end of blanket, work embroidery with a blunt-ended yarn needle in

lazy daisy stitch, French knots, chain stitch or backstitch as foll:

Flowers

Work 2 flowers on top of stems at lower right-hand corner of blanket. Using 2 strands of yarn and 12mm/$\frac{1}{2}$in lazy daisy stitches, work 5 petals for each flower (yarn **C** for flower on short stem and yarn **G** for flower on tall stem). Using 2 strands of yarn **D**, work a French knot at centre of each flower.

Car and wagon

Work details on car and wagon using 2 strands of yarn and chain stitch. Using yarn **F**, work 2 circles at bottom of car for wheels. Work 2 wheels in same way on wagon, using yarn **G**. For chain between car and wagon, work a straight line, using yarn **B**.

Small houses

Using 2 strands of yarn and backstitch, work 4cm/1$\frac{1}{2}$in tall numbers on doors of 3 small houses at lower end of blanket – using yarn **G**, work number '1' on house at left; using yarn **C**, work number '2' on house in middle; and using yarn **B**, work number '3' on house at right.

Using one strand of yarn and backstitch, work crosses on windows to depict 4 window panes – on house '1', use yarn **D** for top centre window and yarn **B** for 3 remaining windows; and on house '3', use yarn **C** for 2 bottom windows and yarn **G** for 4 top windows. On house '2', work 2 vertical and 2 horizontal lines to depict 9 window panes, using one strand of yarn **E**.

Using one strand of yarn and chain stitch, work 2 long wavy lines coming out of each of 2 chimneys to depict smoke. Use yarn **G** for house '1' and yarn **J** for house '3'.

Trees

Work trunks for 5 trees without trunks, using one strand of yarn and working a straight line of chain stitch from lower edge of crown of tree to ground. Starting at bottom of hill, use yarn **H** for trunk on cirlce tree in **J**, yarn **G** for triangle tree in **C**, and yarn **J** for oval tree in **H**. At top of hill, use yarn C for trunk of triangle tree in **F**, and **G** for circle tree in **A**.

Castle

For doorknob on castle at top end of blanket, work a circle, using one strand of yarn **G** and chain stitch. To depict panes on windows, work a cross in backstitch on each window with one strand of yarn, using yarn **G** for 4 windows in **D**, yarn **J** for 2 windows in **B** and one window in **G**, and yarn **B** for 2 windows in **J**. For each flagpole, work a straight line in chain stitch (from lower edge of flag to roof), using yarn **G** for flag at left, yarn **J** for flag in middle and yarn **E** for flag at right. Using same shade as flagpole, work a single lazy daisy stitch at top of each flag for knob at top of flagpole.

FAIRYLAND BLANKET
CHART
TOP/MIDDLE/BOTTOM

chart key

A
B
C
D
E
F
G
H
J
L
M
N

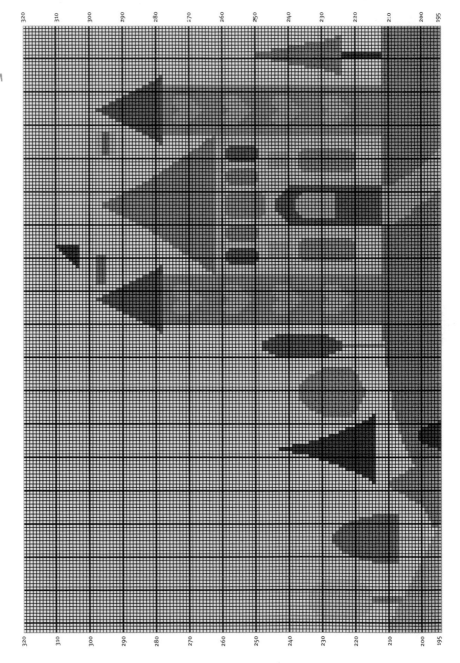

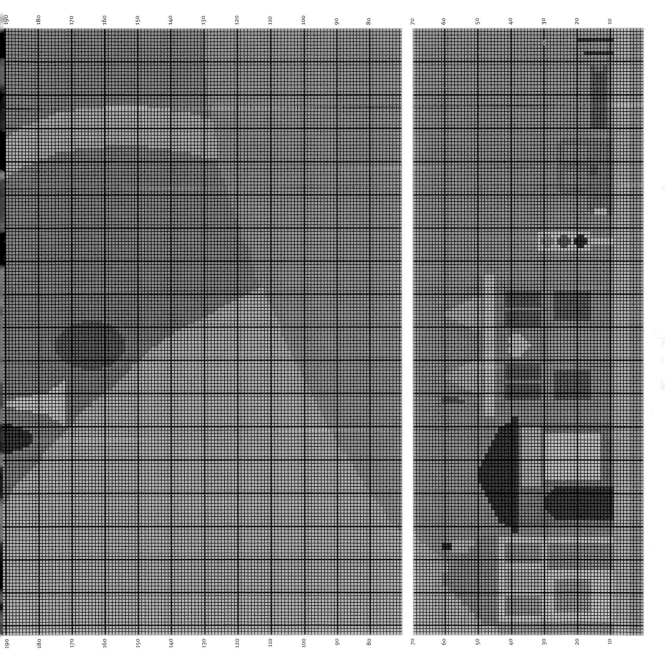

fairy doll

The perfect gift, this fairy doll will give hours of playtime fun to the lucky recipient. You can use leftover yarns to make the doll a full wardrobe of pretty long and short dresses.

SIZE

Finished doll is approximately 37cm/14½in tall.

YARN

Jaeger Matchmaker Merino DK (50g/1¾oz per ball) as foll:

A bright pink/Rock Rose 896, 1 ball
B beige/Soft Camel 865, 1 ball
C mid purple/Parma 888, 1 ball
D pale pink/Petal 883, 1 ball
E cream/Buttermilk 911, 1 ball
F pale baby blue/Feather 864, 1 ball

NEEDLES & EXTRAS

Pair of 4mm (US size 6) knitting needles
Pair of 3¾mm (US size 5) knitting needles
3.50mm (US size E/4) crochet hook
Toy filling

TENSION/GAUGE

22 sts and 30 rows to 10cm/4in measured over st st using 4mm (US size 6) needles.

ABBREVIATIONS

See page 9.

DOLL

Body and head

Trunk of body and head are worked in one piece, starting at lower end of trunk.

Using 4mm (US size 6) needles and yarn **A**, cast on 42 sts.

Beg with a K row, work 10 rows in st st, ending with a WS row.

Break off yarn **A**.

Shape body

Using yarn **B** and cont in st st throughout, work as foll:

Next row (RS) *K5, K2tog, rep from * to end. 36 sts.

Work straight/even for 1 row.

Next row (RS) *K5, K2tog, rep from * to last st, K1. 31 sts.

Work straight/even for 5 rows, ending with a WS row.

Next row (RS) *K4, K2tog, rep from * to last st, K1. 26 sts.

Work straight/even for 3 rows, ending with a WS row.

Next row (RS) [K5, K2tog] 3 times, K5. 23 sts.

Work straight/even for 15 rows, ending with a WS row.

Shape shoulders

Next row (RS) K4, [K2tog] twice, K7, [K2tog] twice, K4. 19 sts.

Work straight/even for 1 row.

Next row (RS) K3, [K2tog] twice, K5, [K2tog] twice, K3. 15 sts.

Work straight/even for 1 row.

Shape neck and head

Next row (RS) *K1, K into front and back of next st, rep from * to last st, K1. 22 sts.

Work straight/even for 1 row.

Next row (RS) K2, K into front and back of next st, K5, K into front and back of next st, K4, K into front and back of next st, K5, K into front and back of next st, K2. 26 sts.

Work straight/even for 15 rows, ending with a WS row.

Shape top of head

Next row (RS) *K3, K2tog, rep from * to last st, K1. 21 sts.

Work straight/even for 1 row.

Next row (RS) *K1, K2tog, rep from * to end. 14 sts.

Next row *P2tog, rep from * to end. 7 sts.

Slip rem 7 sts onto a stitch holder, then break off yarn, leaving a long tail-end to sew back seam.

Legs (make 2)

Using 4mm (US size 6) needles and yarn **C**, cast on 8 sts.

Starting at toe end of leg, work in st st as foll:

Row 1 (RS) *K2, K into front and back of next st, rep from * to last 2 sts, K2. 10 sts.

Row 2 P to end.

Row 3 *K2, K into front and back of next st, rep from * to last st, K1. 13 sts.

Row 4 P to end.

Row 5 *K3, K into front and back of next st, rep from * to last st, K1. 16 sts.

Row 6 P to end.

Row 7 K5, K into front and back of next st, K4, K into front and back of next st, K5. 18 sts.

Cont in st st throughout, work straight/even for 2 rows, ending with a RS row.

Break off yarn **C**.

Using yarn **D**, work straight/even for 45 rows, ending with a WS row.

Cast/bind off.

Arms (make 2)

Using 4mm (US size 6) needles and yarn **B**, cast on 6 sts.

Starting at hand end of arm, work in st st as foll:

Row 1 (RS) K1, K into front and back of next st, K2, K into front and back of next st, K1. 8 sts.

Row 2 P to end.

Row 3 [K2, K into front and back of next st] twice, K2. 10 sts.

Row 4 P to end.

Row 5 [K1, K into front and back of next st] twice, K2, [K into front and back of next st, K1] twice. 14 sts.

Row 6 P to end.

Row 7 K3, K into front and back of next st, K6, K into front and back of next st, K3. 16 sts.

Cont in st st throughout, work straight/even for 3 rows, ending with a WS row.

Break off yarn **B**.

Cont in stripes as foll:

Work 4 rows using yarn **C, work 4 rows using yarn **E**.**

Rep from ** to ** 4 times more, ending with a WS row.

Work 6 rows yarn **C**, ending with a WS row.

Cast/bind off.

TO FINISH

Sew together pieces, then attach hair and work embroidery as foll:

Body

Thread end of yarn onto a blunt-ended yarn needle and pass needle through remaining stitches while slipping them off stitch holder. Pull yarn to gather stitches and secure, then sew centre back seam from top of head to cast-on edge.

Fill body firmly with toy filling and sew opening closed.

Legs

To create a ballet-shoe effect at end of each leg, work 2 lines of chain stitch on each leg just above 'shoes' in yarn **C**. Using a blunt-ended yarn needle and yarn **C**, work first line starting at 'shoe' and between fourth and fifth stitch from right side edge of first leg; continue up leg in a diagonal line, ending above 12th row from 'shoe'. Work a mirror image of this line that crosses it at centre of same leg. Embroider other leg in same way. Sew leg seams, leaving cast/bound-off edge open. Fill each leg firmly with toy filling. Pinch opening together so that leg seam is centred on one side and sew opening closed.

Sew legs to lower edge of body.

Arms

Prepare arms as for legs, then sew ends vertically to sides of body just below neck.

Eyes and mouth

Using a blunt-ended yarn needle and yarn **F**, work two French knots on head for eyes. Then work mouth in backstitch, using yarn **A**.

Hair

Attach hair to doll's head in tufts. For each tuft, cut two 33cm/13in lengths of yarn **D**. Hold two

strands together and fold in half. Then using a crochet hook, draw folded end of first tuft through knitting at top of head along a central parting line. Pull all four tail-ends of tuft through loop at folded end and tighten firmly to form a knot. Work six tufts closely together along each side of central parting, then work six more tufts under these on each side of head to fill out hair. Trim hair to desired length.

Cut two short lengths of yarn **A** and tie hair in bunches at each side of head, 6.5cm/2¹⁄₂in from central parting.

DRESS
To make dress
Using 4mm (US size 6) needles and yarn **A**, cast on 50 sts.

Starting at hem edge, work dress in garter st (K every row) in stripes as foll:
Rows 1–4 Using yarn **A**, K 4 rows.
Rows 5–8 Using yarn **F**, K 4 rows.
(These 8 rows are repeated to form garter st stripe patt.)
Cont in garter st stripe patt as set throughout, work 4 rows more.
Shape skirt
Next row (RS) K5, K2tog, K11, K2tog, K10, K2tog, K11, K2tog, K5. 46 sts.
Work straight/even for 9 rows, ending with a WS row.
Next row (RS) K5, K2tog, K9, K2tog, K10, K2tog, K9, K2tog, K5. 42 sts.
Work straight/even for 5 rows, ending with a WS row.
Next row (RS) K4, K2tog, K9, K2tog, K8, K2tog, K9, K2tog, K4. 38 sts.
Work straight/even for 5 rows, ending with a WS row.
Next row (RS) K4, K2tog, K7, K2tog, K8, K2tog, K7, K2tog, K4. 34 sts.
Work straight/even for 1 row.
Next row (RS) K8, K2tog, K14, K2tog, K8. 32 sts.
Work straight/even for 1 row.
Next row (RS) K7, K2tog, K14, K2tog, K7. 30 sts.
Work straight/even for 11 rows, ending with a WS row. (A total of 50 rows have been completed from cast-on edge.)
Shape top of left back
Next row (RS) K7, then turn, leaving rem sts on a stitch holder.
Work on these 7 sts only for left side of back of dress.

Next row K2tog, K to end. 6 sts.

Work straight/even for 8 rows, ending with a WS row.

Next row (RS) K to last 2 sts, K2tog. 5 sts.

Next row K2tog, K to end. 4 sts.

Next row K to last 2 sts, K2tog.

Cast/bind off rem 3 sts knitwise.

Shape top of front

With RS facing, rejoin yarn to sts on holder, cast/bind off first 2 sts and K until there are 12 sts on right-hand needle, then turn, leaving rem sts on stitch holder.

Work on these 12 sts only for front of dress.

Next row K2tog, K to last 2 sts, K2tog. 10 sts.

Work straight/even for 8 rows, ending with a WS row.

Next row (RS) K4, then turn, leaving rem sts on a second stitch holder.

Work on these 4 sts only for left front neck edge.

Next row K2tog, K to end. 3 sts.

Next row K1, K2tog.

Cast/bind off rem 2 sts knitwise.

With RS facing, rejoin yarn to sts on second holder and cast/bind off first 2 sts, then K to end. 4 sts.

Work on these 4 sts only for right front neck edge.

Next row K to last 2 sts, K2tog. 3 sts.

Next row K2tog, K1.

Cast/bind off rem 2 sts knitwise.

Shape top of right back

With RS facing, rejoin yarn to sts on first holder and cast/bind off first 2 sts, then K to end. 7 sts.

Work on these 7 sts only for right side of back of dress.

Next row K to last 2 sts, K2tog. 6 sts.

Work straight/even for 8 rows, ending with a WS row.

Next row (RS) K2tog, K to end. 5 sts.

Next row K to last 2 sts, K2tog. 4 sts.

Next row K2tog, K to end.

Cast/bind off rem 3 sts knitwise.

TO FINISH

Do NOT press dress.

Armhole edging

With RS facing and using 3¾mm (US size 5) needles and yarn **E**, pick up and knit 18 sts evenly around armhole, casting/binding them off as they are picked up.

Neck edging

Sew shoulder seams.

With RS facing and using 3¾mm (US size 5) needles and yarn **E**, pick up and knit 24 sts evenly along neck edge, casting/binding them off as they are picked up.

Beginning at hem edge, sew centre back seam using mattress st and leaving top 5cm/2in open. For a removable dress, sew a length of yarn **E** to neckline on each side of back opening, put dress on and tie to fasten. For a permanent dress, put dress on doll and complete top of centre back seam.

sea scene hoodie

Knitted in cool cotton, this fun, brightly coloured sweater is just what a little boy or girl needs for cool summer evenings. Embroider the number on the sail to match the wearer's age.

SIZES & MEASUREMENTS

To fit

3–4	4–5	5–6	6–7	years

Knitted measurements

Around chest

70	76	84	90	cm
27½	30	33	35½	in

Length to shoulder

39	41	42.5	44	cm
15¼	16	16¾	17¼	in

Sleeve seam

32	33.5	35	37	cm
12¾	13¼	13¾	14½	in

YARN

Rowan Cotton Rope (50g/1¾oz per ball):
A navy blue/Harbour 068, 3 (3:4: 4) balls
B turquoise/Calypso 064, 3 (4: 4: 4) balls
C white/White 067, 2 (3: 3: 3) balls
D light green/Limeade 065, 1 (1: 1: 1) ball
E orange/Squash 061, 1 (1: 1: 1) ball
F yellow/Lemonade 060, 1 (1: 1: 1) ball

NEEDLES

Pair of 5½mm (US size 9) knitting needles
Pair of 6mm (US size 10) knitting needles

TENSION/GAUGE

16 sts and 23 rows to 10cm/4in measured over st st using 6mm (US size 10) needles.

ABBREVIATIONS

See page 9.

CHART NOTE

Work the chart pattern in stocking/stockinette stitch. Read all odd-numbered (knit) chart rows from right to left and all even-numbered (purl) chart rows from left to right.

Use the intarsia technique for the chart pattern, using a separate length of yarn for each area of colour and twisting the yarns together on the wrong side of the work where they meet.

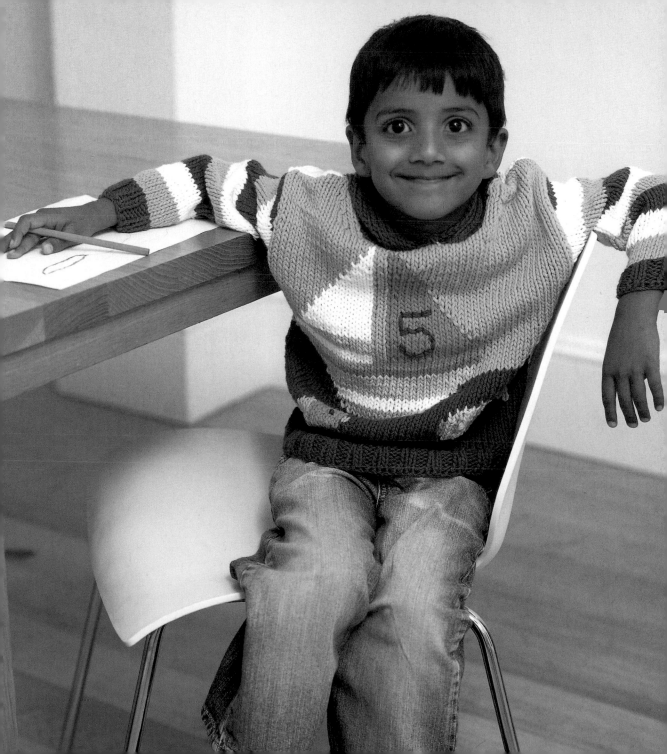

BACK

Using 5½mm (US size 9) needles and yarn **A**, cast on 56 (62: 68: 74) sts.

Rib row 1 (RS) K1 (2: 1: 2), *P2, K2, rep from * to last 3 (4: 3: 4) sts, P2, K1 (2: 1: 2).

Rib row 2 P1 (2: 1: 2), *K2, P2, rep from * to last 3 (4: 3: 4) sts, K2, P1 (2: 1: 2).

Rep last 2 rows twice more.

Break off yarn **A**.**

Change to 6mm (US size 10) needles and yarn **C**.

Beg with a K row, work 36 (38: 40: 42) rows in st st, ending with a WS row.

Shape armholes

Cont in st st throughout, dec 1 st at each end of next row and then foll alt row, ending with a RS row. 52 (58: 64: 70) sts.

Beg with a P row, work straight/even for rows 39 (41: 43: 45) rows, ending with a WS row.

Shape right neck edge and shoulder

Next row (RS) Cast/bind off first 3 (4: 4: 5) sts, K until there are 16 (17: 19: 20) sts on right-hand needle, then turn, leaving rem 33 (37: 41: 45) sts on a stitch holder.

Work on these 16 (17: 19: 20) sts only for right side of neck.

Dec 1 st at beg of next row (neck edge). 15 (16: 18: 19) sts.

Next row (RS) Cast/bind off first 3 (4: 4: 4) sts, K to last 2 sts, K2tog. 11 (11: 13: 14) sts.

Dec 1 st at beg of next row. 10 (10: 12: 13) sts.

Next row (RS) Cast/bind off first 3 (3: 4: 4) sts, K to last 2 sts, K2tog. 6 (6: 7: 8) sts.

P 1 row.

Cast/bind off 3 (3: 4: 4) sts at beg of next row. 3 (3: 3: 4) sts.

P 1 row.

Cast/bind off.

Shape left neck edge and shoulder

With RS facing, rejoin yarn to sts on holder and cast/bind off centre 14 (16: 18: 20) sts, then K to end. 19 (21: 23: 25) sts.

Next row (WS) Cast/bind off first 3 (4: 4: 5) sts, P to last 2 sts, P2tog. 15 (16: 18: 19) sts.

Dec 1 st at beg of next row (neck edge). 14 (15: 17: 18) sts.

Next row (WS) Cast/bind off first 3 (4: 4: 4) sts, P to last 2 sts, P2tog. 10 (10: 12: 13) sts.

Dec 1 st at beg of next row. 9 (9: 11: 12) sts.

Cast/bind off 3 (3: 4: 4) sts at beg of next row. 6 (6: 7: 8) sts.

K 1 row.

Cast/bind off 3 (3: 4: 4) sts at beg of next row.

Cast/ bind off rem 3 (3: 3: 4) sts.

FRONT

Work as for back to **.

Change to 6mm (US size 10) needles.

Beg with a K row (chart row 1), work chart patt in st st – between markers for chosen size – until chart row 36 (38: 40: 42) has been completed, ending with a WS row.

Shape armholes

Cont in st st chart patt throughout, dec 1 st at each end of next row and then foll alt row, ending with a RS row. 52 (58: 64: 70) sts.

Beg with a P row, work straight/even until chart row 72 (76: 80: 84) has been completed, ending with a WS row.

Shape left neck edge and shoulder

Cont in st st with yarn **B** only as foll:

Next row (RS) K21 (23: 25: 27), then turn,

leaving rem 31 (35: 39: 43) sts on a stitch holder.

Work on these 21 (23: 25: 27) sts only for left side of neck.

Dec 1 st at beg of next row (neck edge). 20 (22: 24: 26) sts.

Dec 1 st at end of next row.

P 1 row.

Rep last 2 rows once more, ending with a WS row. 18 (20: 22: 24) sts.

Next row (RS) Cast/bind off first 3 (4: 4: 5) sts, K to last 2 sts, K2tog. 14 (15: 17: 18) sts.

P 1 row.

Next row (RS) Cast/bind off first 3 (4: 4: 4) sts, K to last 2 sts, K2tog. 10 (10: 12: 13) sts.

P 1 row.

Next row (RS) Cast/bind off first 3 (3: 4: 4) sts, K to last 2 sts, K2tog. 6 (6: 7: 8) sts.

P 1 row.

Cast/bind off 3 (3: 4: 4) sts at beg of next row. 3 (3: 3: 4) sts.

P 1 row.

Cast/bind off.

Shape right neck edge and shoulder

With RS facing, rejoin yarn to sts on holder and cast/bind off centre 10 (12: 14: 16) sts, then K to end. 21 (23: 25: 27) sts.

Dec 1 st at end of next row (neck edge). 20 (22: 24: 26) sts.

Dec 1 st at beg of next row.

P 1 row.

Rep last 2 rows once more, ending with a WS row. 18 (20: 22: 24) sts.

Dec 1 st at beg of next row.

Cast/bind off 3 (4: 4: 5) sts at beg of next row. 14 (15: 17: 18) sts.

Dec 1 st at beg of next row.

Cast/bind off 3 (4: 4: 4) sts at beg of next row. 10 (10: 12: 13) sts.

Dec 1 st at beg of next row.

Cast/bind off first 3 (3: 4: 4) sts at beg of next row. 6 (6: 7: 8) sts.

K 1 row.

Cast/bind off first 3 (3: 4: 4) sts at beg of next row.

Cast/bind off rem 3 (3: 3: 4) sts.

SLEEVES (make 2)

Using 5½mm (US size 9) needles and yarn **A**, cast on 30 (34: 38: 42) sts.

Rib row 1 (RS) *K2, P2, rep from * to last 2 sts, K2.

Rib row 2 *P2, K2, rep from * to last 2 sts, P2.

Rep last 2 rows twice more.

Change to 6mm (US size 10) needles.

Beg with a K row (chart row 1), work chart patt in st st – between markers for chosen size – until chart row 51 has been completed and at the same time inc 1 st at each end of third row and then every foll sixth row 8 times, ending with a RS row. 48 (52: 56: 60) sts.

Cont chart patt in st st throughout, work straight/even for 7 (11: 15: 19) rows, ending with a WS row.

Shape top of sleeve

Dec 1 st at each end of next 4 rows, ending with a WS row. 40 (44: 48: 52) sts.

Cast/bind off 3 (4: 4: 5) sts at beg of next 2 rows. 34 (36: 40: 42) sts.

Cast/bind off 3 (4: 4: 4) sts at beg of next 2 rows. 28 (28: 32: 34) sts.

Cast/bind off 3 (3: 4: 4) sts at beg of next 4 rows. 16 (16: 16: 18) sts.

Cast/bind off 3 (3: 3: 4) sts at beg of next 2 rows.

Cast/bind off rem 10 sts.

CENTRE STRIP OF HOOD

Using 6mm (US size 10) needles and yarn **B**, cast on 12 sts.

Beg with a K row, work in st st in stripes as foll:
6 rows in yarn **B**, 6 rows yarn **A** and 6 rows in yarn **C**.

Rep from *** to *** 3 times more.

Cont in st st, work 0 (2: 4: 6) rows in yarn **B**.

Cast/ bind off.

RIGHT SIDE OF HOOD

Using 6mm (US size 10) needles and yarn **A**, cast on 17 (19: 21: 23) sts.

Beg at top end of hood piece and working to-wards neck edge end, shape piece as foll:

Row 1 (RS) K into front and back of first st, K to end. 18 (20: 22: 24) sts.

Row 2 P to last st, P into front and back of last st. 19 (21: 23: 25) sts.

Row 3 K into front and back of first st, K to end. 20 (22: 24: 26) sts.

Row 4 P to end.

Rep last 2 rows 3 times more. 23 (25: 27: 29) sts.

Cont in st st throughout and keeping left edge of piece straight, inc 1 st at beg of next row and then at beg of every foll sixth row 4 (4: 4: 3) times, ending with a RS row. 28 (30: 32: 33) sts.

Work another 7 (7: 7: 15) rows straight in st st, ending with a WS row.

Mark end of last row with a contrasting yarn.

Dec 1 st at beg of next row and then at beg of 5 (6: 7: 7) foll alt rows ending with a RS row. 22 (23: 24: 25) sts.

P 1 row.

Cast/bind off 11 (11: 12: 12) sts at beg of next row.

Cast/ bind off rem 11 (12: 12: 13) sts.

LEFT SIDE OF HOOD

Using 6mm (US size 10) needles and yarn **A**, cast on 17 (19: 21: 23) sts.

Beg at top end of hood piece and working towards neck edge end, shape piece as foll:

Row 1 (RS) K to last st, K into front and back of last st. 18 (20: 22: 24) sts.

Row 2 P into front and back of first st, P to end. 19 (21: 23: 25) sts.

Row 3 K to last st, K into front and back of last st. 20 (22: 24: 26) sts.

Row 4 P to end.

Rep last 2 rows 3 times more. 23 (25: 27: 29) sts.

Cont in st st throughout and keeping right edge of piece straight, inc 1 st at end of next row and then at end of every foll sixth row 4 (4: 4: 3) times,

ending with a RS row. 28 (30: 32: 33) sts.

Work another 7 (7: 7: 15) rows straight in st st, ending with a WS row.

Mark beg of last row with a contrasting yarn.

Dec 1 st at end of next row and then at end of 5 (6: 7: 7) foll alt rows ending with a RS row. 22 (23: 24: 25) sts.

Cast/bind off 11 (11: 12: 12) sts at beg of next row.

Cast/ bind off rem 11 (12: 12: 13) sts.

HOOD EDGING

Using 5¹⁄₂mm (US size 9) needles and yarn **A**, cast on 66 (70: 74: 78) sts.

Rib row 1 (RS) *K2, P2, rep from * to last 2 sts, K2.

Rib row 2 *P2, K2, rep from * to last 2 sts, P2.

Rep last 2 rows twice more

Cast/bind off knitwise.

TO FINISH

Press pieces lightly on WS following instructions on yarn label and avoiding ribbing.

Weave in all loose ends.

Striped hood centre fits along cast-on edge of hood pieces and along shaped edge, ending at markers. First, pin side edges of striped centre of hood to hood pieces, aligning cast-on edge of hood centre with straight side edge of hood pieces and each end of cast/bound-off edge of hood centre with a marker. Then sew pieces together.

Pin then sew hood edging to straight edges of side hood pieces and cast-on edge of hood centre.

Sew both shoulder seams.

Sew hood to neck edge, overlapping hood edging at centre front neck edge.

Fold top of each sleeve in half to find centre and mark with a pin. Sew sleeves to armholes, matching centre of top of sleeve to shoulder seam.

Sew side and sleeve seams.

Embroidery

Use a blunt-ended yarn needle for embroidery. Using yarn **A**, embroider child's age in backstitch on orange sail. Work a French knot on each fish for an eye, using yarn **A** for orange fish and yarn **B** for green-and-yellow striped fish.

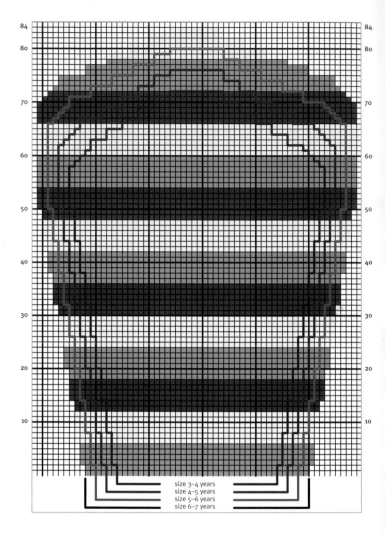

size 3–4 years
size 4–5 years
size 5–6 years
size 6–7 years

SEA SCENE HOODIE CHART
SLEEVE

chart key

■ A
▨ B
□ C

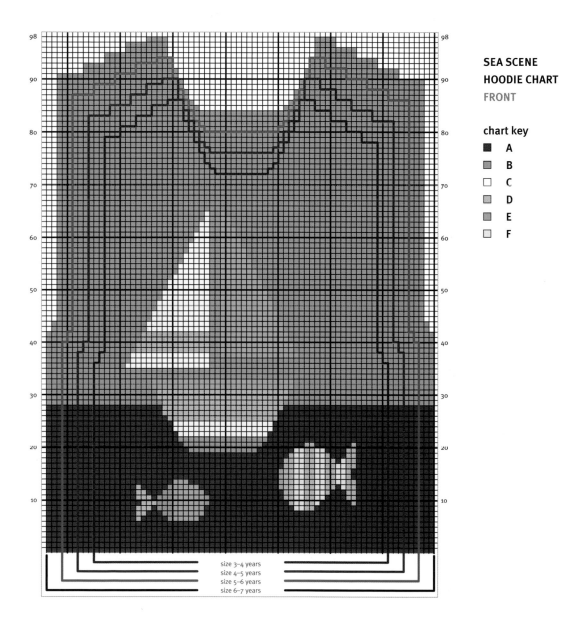

**SEA SCENE
HOODIE CHART**

FRONT

chart key

■	A
■	B
□	C
■	D
■	E
□	F

size 3–4 years
size 4–5 years
size 5–6 years
size 6–7 years

alpine blanket

This alpine scene blanket with embroidered details will inspire the imaginations of tiny tots playing with their toys. Knit it to accompany the toy truck on page 116.

SIZE

Finished blanket measures approximately 95cm/37½in by 120cm/47¼in, including edging.

YARN

Jaeger Matchmaker Merino DK (50g/1¾oz per ball) as foll:

A light yellow-green/Hop 899, 2 balls

B white/White 661, 2 balls

C cherry red/Cherry 656, 2 balls

D camel/Soft Camel 865, 1 ball

E dark brown/Bison 728, 1 ball

F dark green/Loden 730, 2 balls

G dark grey/Charcoal 783, 2 balls

H dark steel blue/Mariner 629, 2 balls

J light grey/Flannel 782, 2 balls

L burnt orange/Pumpkin 898, 2 balls

N pale baby blue/Feather 864, 2 balls

O light green/Sage 857, 2 balls

Q dark olive green/Olive 912, 1 ball

NEEDLES

Pair of 4mm (US size 6) knitting needles

TENSION/GAUGE

22 sts and 30 rows to 10cm/4in measured over st st chart patt using 4mm (US size 6) needles.

ABBREVIATIONS

See page 9.

CHART NOTE

Work the chart pattern in stocking/stockinette stitch. Read all odd-numbered (knit) chart rows from right to left and all even-numbered (purl) chart rows from left to right.

Use the intarsia technique for the chart pattern, using a separate length of yarn for each area of colour and twisting the yarns together on the wrong side of the work where they meet.

TO MAKE BLANKET

Using 4mm (US size 6) needles and yarn **A**, cast on 182 sts.

Beg with a K row (chart row 1), work chart patt in st st until row 340 has been completed, ending with a WS row. Cast/bind off.

EDGING STRIPS (make 4)

Using 4mm (US size 6) needles and yarn **F**, cast on 2 sts.

Work first edging strip in garter st (K every row) as foll:

Row 1 (WS) K to end.

Row 2 (inc row) (RS) K into front and back of first st, K to end. 3 sts.

Rows 3–28 Rep rows 1 and 2 thirteen times. 16 sts.

Mark beg of last row with a contrasting yarn. Work straight/even in garter st until strip between marker and needle fits across top edge of blanket, ending with a WS row.

Shape other end of strip on same edge as first end as foll:

Next row (dec row) (RS) K2tog, K to end. 15 sts.

Next row K to end.

Rep last 2 rows 12 times, ending with a WS row. 3 sts.

Next row (dec row) (RS) K2tog, K1.

Cast/bind off rem 2 sts knitwise.

Work edging strips for other three sides of blanket in same way, but using yarn **L** for bottom strip, yarn **H** for left side edge, and yarn **C** for right side edge.

TO FINISH

Press blanket lightly on WS following instructions on yarn label. Do NOT press edging strips.

Pin each edging strip (between increase and decrease rows) to edge of blanket and sew in place.

Sew together diagonal ends of edging strips at corners of blanket.

Work embroidery next.

EMBROIDERY

Houses

To depict panes on window panes, work a cross in backstitch on each window – on house at lower end of blanket, use yarn **H** on lowest window, yarns **C**, **E** and **L** on 3 middle windows from left to right, and yarn **H** on top window; on window of house in middle of blanket, use yarn **C**. For smoke, work 2 long wavy lines in chain stitch coming out of each of 2 chimneys, using yarn **G**.

Trees

For snow on trees, work chain stitch in yarn **B** on top and first branch of tree in yarn **Q** next to house at lower end of blanket. Work snow in same way on tree in **Q** at left of house at middle of blanket and tree in **F** at right of same house, then on top of a few of trees in **Q** on horizon.

Cars and truck

For light beams, work 3 long straight lines of backstitch in yarn **L**, radiating out of headlight of cars and truck.

Road

For road dividing line, work a broken line of backstitch down middle of road using yarn **B**.

ALPINE BLANKET CHART

TOP/MIDDLE/BOTTOM

chart key

A
B
C
D
E
F
G
H
J
L
N
O
Q

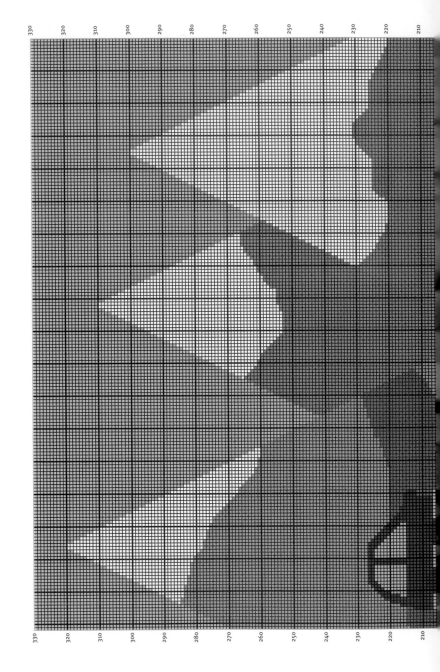

toy truck

Little hands will enjoy driving this knitted toy truck up the road on the Alpine Blanket on page 110. Use the recommended machine-washable wool yarn or make it with leftover yarns.

SIZE
Finished truck measures approximately 22cm/8¾in long by 8cm/3in wide by 13.5cm/5¼in tall.

YARN
Jaeger Matchmaker Merino DK (50g/1¾oz per ball):

A navy blue/Mid Navy 2346; 1 ball
B cherry red/Cherry 656; 1 ball
C burnt orange/Pumpkin 898; 1 ball
D dark grey/Charcoal 783; 1 ball
E dark steel blue/Mariner 629; 1 ball
F light yellow-green/Hop 899; 1 ball
G light grey/Flannel 782; 1 ball

NEEDLES & EXTRAS
Pair of 4mm (US size 6) knitting needles
Iron-on interfacing
Toy filling

TENSION/GAUGE
22 sts and 30 rows to 10cm/4in measured over st st chart patt using 4mm (US size 6) needles.

ABBREVIATIONS
See page 9.

CHART NOTE
Work the chart patterns in stocking/stockinette stitch. Read all odd-numbered (knit) chart rows from right to left and all even-numbered (purl) chart rows from left to right.

Use the intarsia technique for the chart patterns, using a separate length of yarn for each area of colour and twisting the yarns together on the wrong side of the work where they meet.

TOP AND BOTTOM OF TRUCK

Top, bottom, front and back of truck are
worked in one strip in st st.

Using 4mm (US size 6) and yarn **A**, cast on 17
sts.

Back of truck

Starting at back of truck and breaking off and
joining in yarns as needed, work in st st as foll:
Beg with a K row, work 2 rows in st st, ending
with a WS row.

Beg with a K row (chart row 1), work in st st
from chart for BACK OF TRUCK until chart row
9 has been completed, ending with a RS row.
Cont with yarn **A** only and beg with a P row,
work 23 rows in st st, ending with a WS row.

Top of truck

Work top of truck in st st stripes as foll:
**Beg with a K row, work 5 rows in st st using
yarn **D**, then 5 rows using yarn **C**, ending with a
WS row.**

Rep from ** to ** 3 times more, ending with a
WS row.

Beg with a K row, work 5 rows in st st using
yarn **D**, ending with a RS row.

Front of truck

Cont in st st and beg with a P row, work 23
rows in yarn **B**, 2 rows in yarn **D**, 10 rows in
yarn **E**, 2 rows in yarn **D**, and 4 rows in yarn **B**,
ending with a WS row.

Beg with a K row (chart row 1), work in st st
from chart for FRONT OF TRUCK until chart row
6 has been completed, ending with a WS row.
Cont in st st and beg with a K row, work 6 rows
in yarn **B**, ending with a WS row.

Bottom of truck

Work bottom of first set of wheels in garter st

(K every row) as foll:

***[Using yarn **D**, K 2 rows, then using yarn **G**, K 2 rows] 4 times.

Using yarn **D**, K 2 rows, ending with a WS row.***

This completes bottom of first wheel.

Using yarn **B** and beg with a K row, work 4 rows in st st, ending with a WS row.

Using yarn **A** and beg with a K row, work 4 rows in st st, ending with a WS row.

Rep from *** to *** for bottom of second set of wheels.

Using yarn **A** and beg with a K row, work 12 rows in st st, ending with a WS row.

Rep from *** to *** for bottom of third set of wheels.

Using yarn **A** and beg with a K row, work 4 rows in st st, ending with a WS row.

Still using yarn **A**, cast/bind off.

SIDE A OF TRUCK

Work bottom of wheels first before beg to work from chart.

Truck wheels (make 3)

Using 4mm (US size 6) needles and yarn **D**, cast on 3 sts.

Row 1 (RS) K3.

Beg with a P row, work in st st, inc 1 st at each end of next row and then 2 foll alt rows, ending with a WS row. 9 sts.

Break off yarn **D** and slip these 9 sts onto a stitch holder.

Make 2 more wheels in same way and transfer them both onto same stitch holder with same sides facing.****

Join wheels to side of truck

Using 4mm (US size 6) needles and yarn **A**, cast on 3 sts onto RH needle; with WS facing, slip 9 sts of one wheel onto RH needle; using a separate length of yarn **A**, cast on 9 sts onto RH needle; slip 9 sts of second wheel onto needle; using a separate length of yarn **A**, cast on 3 sts, then using a length of yarn **B**, cast on 3 sts; slip 9 sts of third wheel onto needle; using a length of yarn **B**, cast on 3 sts. 48 sts.

Work chart row 7 across all sts on needle as foll:

Chart row 7 (RS) K3 using yarn **B**, K9 using yarn **D**, K3 using yarn **B**, K33 using yarn **A**.

Beg with chart row 8 (a P row), work in st st from the chart for the side of the truck until chart row 40 has been completed, shaping front of truck as indicated and ending with a WS row.

Using yarn **A**, cast/bind off.

SIDE B OF TRUCK

Work as for Side A of truck to ****.

Join wheels to side of truck

Using 4mm (US size 6) needles and yarn **B**, cast on 3 sts onto RH needle; with WS facing, slip 9 sts of one wheel onto RH needle; using a separate length of yarn **B**, cast on 3 sts onto RH needle, then using a length of yarn **A**, cast on 3 sts; slip 9 sts of second wheel onto RH needle; using a separate length of yarn **A**, cast on 9 sts; slip 9 sts of third wheel onto RH needle; using a length of yarn **A**, cast on 3 sts. 48 sts.

Work chart row 7 across all sts on needle as a mirror image of the other side as foll:

Chart row 7 (RS) K33 using yarn **A**, K3 using yarn **B**, K9 using yarn **D**, K3 using yarn **B**.

Complete as for the first side, reversing colours and shaping.

TO FINISH

Press pieces lightly on WS following instructions on yarn label and avoiding garter st.

Cut and iron interfacing fabric onto WS of each of pieces of truck, allowing 12mm/½in extra all around edged for seams.

Sew sides of truck to top-and-bottom strip, matching wheels and rear and front lights – and leaving an opening for inserting filling.

Fill firmly with toy filling and sew opening closed.

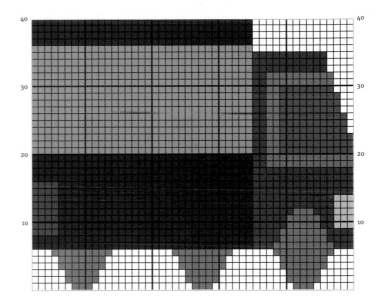

TOY TRUCK CHART
FRONT LIGHTS

chart key
- ■ B
- ■ C
- ☐ F

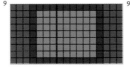

TOY TRUCK CHART
BACK LIGHTS

chart key
- ■ A
- ■ B
- ■ C

TOY TRUCK
CHART SIDE

chart key
- ■ A
- ■ B
- ■ C
- ■ D
- ■ E
- ☐ F
- ■ G

TEXTURED KNITS

cute bobble cardigan

Inspired by traditional Aran designs, this knit illustrates the time-less beauty of the old techniques. The simple embroidery is worked in lazy daisy stitch, straight stitch and French knots.

SIZES & MEASUREMENTS
To fit

4–5	5–6	6–7	years

Knitted measurements
Around chest

64	70	78	cm
$25^1/_4$	$27^1/_2$	$30^1/_4$	in

Length to shoulder

33	36	38	cm
13	$14^1/_4$	15	in

Sleeve length

25	31	32	cm
$9^3/_4$	$12^1/_4$	$12^3/_4$	in

YARN
Cardigan
9 (9: 10) 100g/$3^1/_2$oz balls of Rowan
  Scottish Tweed Aran in **A** (off-white/
  Porridge 024)
One 50g/$1^3/_4$oz ball of Jaeger Matchmaker
  Merino DK in **B** (dusty pink/Rosy 870)

Embroidery
Use leftover medium-weight wool yarns
for embroidery **or** purchase one 50g/$1^3/_4$oz
ball each of Jaeger Matchmaker Merino DK
in **C** (plum/Burgundy 655), **D** (pale pink/Petal
883), **E** (pale baby blue/Feather 864), **F** (light
yellow-green/Hop 899) and **G** (dark
green/Loden 730)

NEEDLES & EXTRAS
Pair of 8mm (US size 11) knitting needles
Pair of $7^1/_2$mm (US size $10^1/_2$) knitting needles
6mm (US size 10) circular knitting needle
Cable needle
6 wooden toggle buttons

TENSION/GAUGE
12 sts and 16 rows to 10cm/4in measured over
st st using 8mm (US size 11) needles.

ABBREVIATIONS
MB (make bobble) work [K1, P1, K1, P1, K1, P1,
K1] all into next st, then use tip of left-hand
needle to lift up 2nd, 3rd, 4th, 5th, 6th and 7th
sts one at a time and pass each one over first st
and off right-hand needle.
Also see page 9.

BACK

Using $7\frac{1}{2}$ mm (US size $10\frac{1}{2}$) needles and yarn **A**, cast on 39 (43: 47) sts.

Rib row 1 (RS) *K1, P1, rep from * to last st, K1.

Rib row 2 *P1, K1, rep from * to last st, P1.

Rep last 2 rows twice more, ending with a WS row.

Change to 8mm (US size 11) needles.

Beg with a P row (RS), work 28 (30: 32) rows in rev st st, ending with a WS row.

Shape armholes

Cont in rev st st throughout, dec 1 st at each end of next row.

Work straight/even for 1 row.

Dec 1 st at each end of next row.

Work straight/even for 13 (15: 17) rows, ending with a WS row.

Shape right neck edge and shoulder

Next row (RS) P11 (12: 13), then turn, leaving rem 24 (27: 30) sts on a stitch holder. Work on these 11 (12: 13) sts only for right side of neck.

Dec 1 st at beg of next row (neck edge).

Cast/bind off 5 (5: 6) sts at beg of next row.

Cast/bind off rem 5 (6: 6) sts.

Shape left neck edge and shoulder

With RS facing, rejoin yarn to sts on holder and cast/bind off centre 13 (15: 17) sts, then P to end.

Dec 1 st at end of next row (neck edge).

Cast/bind off 5 (5: 6) sts at end of next row.

Rejoin yarn and cast/bind off rem 5 (6 :6) sts.

RIGHT FRONT

Using $7\frac{1}{2}$mm (US size $10\frac{1}{2}$) needles and yarn **A, cast on 19 (21: 23) sts.

Work 6 rows in K1, P1 rib as for back, ending with a WS row.

Change to 8mm (US size 11) needles.

Beg with a P (RS) row, work 1 (3: 5) rows in rev st st, ending with a RS row.**

Begin cable pattern

Beg cable patt as foll:

Row 1 (WS) K8 (9: 10), P2, K1, P2, K6 (7: 8).

Row 2 (RS) P6 (7: 8), C5B, P8 (9: 10).

Row 3 and all foll WS (odd-numbered) rows K all K sts and P all P sts.

Row 4 P5 (6: 7), C3b, P1, C3f, P7 (8: 9).

Row 6 P4 (5: 6), C3b, P1, MB, P1, C3f, P6 (7: 8).

Row 8 P3 (4: 5), C3b, (P1, MB) twice, P1, C3f, P5 (6: 7).

Row 10 P2 (3: 4), C3b, (P1, MB) 3 times, P1, C3f, P4 (5: 6).

Row 12 P2 (3: 4), K2, P9, K2, P4 (5: 6).

(These 12 rows are repeated to form cable patt.)

Rows 12–24 Rep rows 1–12.

Rows 25–27 Rep rows 1–3.

Shape armhole

Keeping cable patt correct as set, dec 1 st at end of next row. 18 (20: 22) sts.

Work straight/even for 1 row.

Dec 1 st at end of next row. 17 (19: 21) sts.

Work straight/even for 6 rows, ending with a RS row.

This completes cable patt panel.

Beg with a K (WS) row, work 3 (5: 7) rows in rev st st, ending with a WS row.

Shape neck edge and shoulder

Beg with a P (RS) row and cont in rev st st throughout, cast/bind off 4 (5: 6) sts at beg of next row (neck edge). 13 (14: 15) sts.

Dec 1 st at end of next row. 12 (13: 14) sts.

Dec 1 st at beg of next row. 11 (12: 13) sts.

Work straight/even for 1 row.

Dec 1 st at beg of next row. 10 (11: 12) sts.

Work straight/even for 1 row.

Cast/bind off 5 (5: 6) sts at end of next row.
Rejoin yarn and cast/bind off rem 5 (6: 6) sts.

LEFT FRONT

Work as for right front from ** to **.

Beg cable pattern

Beg cable patt as foll:

Row 1 (WS) K6 (7: 8), P2, K1, P2, K8 (9: 10).

Row 2 (RS) P8 (9: 10), C5b, P6 (7: 8).

Row 3 and all foll WS (odd-numbered) rows K all K sts and P all P sts.

Row 4 P7 (8: 9), C3b, P1, C3f, P5 (6: 7).

Row 6 P6 (7: 8), C3b, P1, MB, P1, C3f, P4 (5: 6).

Row 8 P5 (6: 7), C3b, (P1, MB) twice, P1, C3f, P3 (4: 5).

Row 10 P4 (5: 6), C3b, (P1, MB) 3 times, P1, C3f, P2 (3: 4).

Row 12 (RS) P4 (5: 6), K2, P9, K2, P2 (3: 4). (These 12 rows are repeated to form cable patt.)

Rows 12–24 Rep rows 1–12.

Rows 25–27 Rep rows 1–3.

Shape armhole

Keeping cable patt correct as set, dec 1 st at beg of next row. 18 (20: 22) sts.

Work straight/even for 1 row.

Dec 1 st at beg of next row. 17 (19: 21) sts.

Work straight/even for 6 rows, ending with a RS row.

This completes cable patt panel.

Beg with a K (WS) row, work 3 (5: 7) rows in rev st st, ending with a WS row.

Shape neck edge and shoulder

Beg with a P (RS) row and cont in rev st st throughout, cast/bind off 4 (5: 6) sts at end of next row (neck edge). 13 (14: 15) sts.

Rejoin yarn and dec 1 st at beg of next row. 12 (13: 14) sts.

Dec 1 st at end of next row. 11 (12: 13) sts.

Work straight/even for 1 row.

Dec 1 st at end of next row. 10 (11: 12) sts.

Work straight/even for 1 row.

Cast/bind off 5 (5: 6) sts at beg of next row.

Cast/bind off rem 5 (6: 6) sts.

SLEEVES (make 2)

Using 7½mm (US size 10½) needles and 2 strands of yarn **B** held together, cast on 23 (25: 27) sts. (Note: Use one end of yarn from centre of ball and one from outside of ball.) Break off yarn **B**.

Using one strand of yarn **A**, work 6 rows in K1, P1 rib as for back.

Begin cable pattern panel

Change to 8mm (US 11 needles) and work cable patt as foll:

Row 1 (RS) P9 (10: 11), K2, P1, K2, P9 (10: 11).

Row 2 and all foll WS (even-numbered) rows K all K sts and P all P sts.

Row 3 (inc row) P into front and back of first st, P8 (9: 10), C5B, P8 (9: 10), P into front and back of last st. 25 (27: 29) sts.

Row 5 P9 (10: 11), C3b, P1, C3f, P9 (10: 11).

Row 7 P8 (9: 10), C3b, P1, MB, P1, C3f, P8 (9: 10).

Row 9 (inc row) P into front and back of first st, P6 (7: 8), C3b, (P1, MB) twice, P1, C3f, P6 (7: 8), P into front and back of last st. 27 (29: 31) sts.

Row 11 P7 (8: 9), C3b, (P1, MB) 3 times, P1, C3f, P7 (8: 9).

Row 13 (RS) P7 (8: 9), K2, P9, K2, P7 (8: 9).

This completes cable patt panel.

Beg with a K (WS) row, work in rev st st, inc 1 st at each end of 2nd row, and then at each end of 6 foll alt rows, ending with a RS row.

41 (43: 45) sts.

Cont in rev st st throughout, work straight/
even for 5 (11: 17) rows, ending with a WS row.

Shape top of sleeve

Cast/bind off 3 sts (purlwise) at beg of next row.

Cast off 3 sts (knitwise) at beg of next row.

35 (37: 39) sts.

Rep last 2 rows 5 times.

Cast/bind off rem 5 (7: 9) sts.

BUTTON BAND

Using 7$\frac{1}{2}$mm (US size 10$\frac{1}{2}$) needles and yarn
A, cast on 6 sts.

Row 1 (RS) P1, K4, P1.

Row 2 (WS) K1, P4, K1.

(These 2 rows are repeated to form button
band patt.)

Rep rows 1 and 2 until a total of 42 (47: 52)
rows have been completed from cast-on edge,
ending with a WS row.

Cast/bind off in patt.

BUTTONHOLE BAND

Using 7$\frac{1}{2}$mm (US size 10$\frac{1}{2}$) needles and yarn
A, cast on 6 sts.

Row 1 (RS) P1, K4, P1.

Row 2 (WS) K1, P4, K1.

(These 2 rows are repeated to form buttonhole
band patt.)

Keeping patt correct as set, cont as foll:

***Buttonhole row 1** Work first 2 sts in patt, cast/
bind off next 2 sts in patt, work in patt to end.

Buttonhole row 2 Work first 2 sts in patt, cast
on 2 sts, work last 2 sts in patt.

Work 5 (6: 7) rows in patt.***

Rep between *** and *** 4 times more.

Rep buttonhole rows 1 and 2.

Work 3 rows in patt.

Cast/bind off in patt.

Front and neck edging

Using mattress st sew together the shoulder
seams and attach the button bands to the
edges of the fronts of the cardigan, with the
top of the button band matching the point
where the cast off sts for the neck shaping
begins. Using a 6 mm circular needle pick
up 42 (46:50) sts up the edge of the right
button band, pick up 5 sts along the top of the
buttonband, pick up 16 (17:18) sts up the right
front neck, pick up 17 (19:21) sts along back
neck, pick up 16 (17:18) sts down the left front
neck, pick up 5 sts along the top of the button
band and 42 (46:50) sts down the edge of the
left button band. There should be 143 (155:167)
sts on the circular needle.

Using 2 ends of Jaeger Matchmaker Merino DK
Rosy, attach yarn to the back of work at the
bottom of the left button band, with RS of work
facing knit 1 row, turn (WS) and knit a 2nd row,
turn (RS) and cast/bind off knitwise.

Sew in all ends. Fold the sleeves in half and
match the centre fold point with the shoulder
seam, pin and then using mattress stitch sew
the sleeves in position, now sew up the side
and shoulder seams.

Sew on buttons to left button band.

EMBROIDERY

Press pieces lightly on WS following
instructions on yarn label and avoiding cable
patt and ribbing.

Work embroidery using a blunt-ended yarn
needle, 2 strands of yarn and lazy daisy stitch,
straight stitch or French knots.

tammy hat

Knitted in tweed yarn with pretty embroidery, this classic Scottish design still looks great today. Knit it to accessorize the Cute Bobble Cardigan on page 122.

SIZES

To fit

2–3   4–5   6–7   years

YARN

Hat

1 (1: 2) 50g/1¾oz balls of Rowan Scottish
   Tweed DK in **A** (light blue/Skye 003)

Embroidery

Use leftover medium-weight wool yarns for
embroidery **or** purchase one 50g/1¾oz ball
each of Jaeger Matchmaker Merino DK in **B**
(white/White 661), **C** (pale pink/Petal 883), **D**
(dark teal/Teal 790) and **E** (bright pink/Rock
Rose 896)

NEEDLES

Pair of 4mm (US size 6) knitting needles

TENSION/GAUGE

21 sts and 29 rows to 10cm/4in measured over
st st using 4mm (US size 6) needles.

ABBREVIATIONS

See page 9.

TO MAKE HAT

Using 4mm (US size 6) needles and yarn **A**,
cast on 93 (103: 103) sts.

Rib row 1 (RS) *K1, P1, rep from * to last st, K1.

Rib row 2 *P1, K1, rep from * to last st, P1.

Rep last 2 rows twice more.

Beg patt as foll:

Row 1 (RS) K to end.

Row 2 P to end.

Row 3 K4, [yf, K10, yf, K5 (7: 7)] 5 times, yf,
K10, yf, K4. 105 (115: 115) sts.

Row 4 P to end.

Row 5 K4, [yf, K12, yf, K5 (7: 7)] 5 times, yf,
K12, yf, K4. 117 (127: 127) sts.

Row 6 P to end.

Row 7 K4, [yf, K14, yf, K5 (7: 7)] 5 times, yf,
K14, yf, K4. 129 (139: 139) sts.

Row 8 P to end.

Row 9 K4, [yf, K16, yf, K5 (7: 7)] 5 times, yf,
K16, yf, K4. 141 (151: 151) sts.

Row 10 P to end.

For size 2–3 years only

Knit 1 row, purl 1 row, then skip to row 19.

For size 4–5 years only

[Knit 1 row, purl 1 row] 3 times, then skip to
row 19.

For size 6–7 years only

Work rows 11–18 for size 6–7 years only as foll:

Row 11 K4, [yf, K18, yf, K7] 5 times, yf, K18, yf,
K4. – (–: 163) sts.

Rows 12–16 Beg with a P row, work 5 rows in
st st.

Row 17 K2, [skp, K20, K2tog, K3] 5 times, skp,
K20, K2tog, K2. – (–: 151) sts.

Row 18 P to end.

For all sizes

Cont all sizes as foll:

Row 19 (RS) K2, [skp, K18, K2tog, K1 (3: 3)] 5 times, skp, K18, K2tog, K2. 129 (139: 139) sts.

Row 20 and all foll WS (even-numbered) rows P to end.

Row 21 K2, [skp, K16, K2tog, K1 (3: 3)] 5 times, skp, K16, K2tog, K2. 117 (127: 127) sts.

Row 23 K2, [skp, K14, K2tog, K1 (3: 3)] 5 times, skp, K14, K2tog, K2. 105 (115: 115) sts.

Row 25 K2, [skp, K12, K2tog, K1 (3: 3)] 5 times, skp, K12, K2tog, K2. 93 (103: 103) sts.

Row 27 K2, [skp, K10, K2tog, K1 (3: 3)] 5 times, skp, K10, K2tog, K2. 81 (91: 91) sts.

Row 29 K2, [skp, K8, K2tog, K1 (3: 3)] 5 times, skp, K8, K2tog, K2. 69 (79: 79) sts.

Row 31 K2, [skp, K6, K2tog, K1 (3: 3)] 5 times, skp, K6, K2tog, K2. 57 (67: 67) sts.

Row 33 K2, [skp, K4, K2tog, K1 (3: 3)] 5 times, skp, K4, K2tog, K2. 45 (55: 55) sts.

Row 35 K2, [skp, K2, K2tog, K1 (3: 3)] 5 times, skp, K2, K2tog, K2. 33 (43: 43) sts.

Row 37 K2, [skp, K2tog, K1 (3: 3)] 5 times, skp, K2tog, K2. 21 (31: 31) sts.

Row 39 *K2tog, rep from * to last st, K1. 11 (15: 15) sts.

Row 40 P1 (0: 0), *P2tog, rep from * to end. Leaving rem 6 (7: 7) sts on needle, break off yarn, leaving a long tail-end to sew hat seam.

TO FINISH

Thread end of yarn onto a yarn needle and pass needle through remaining stitches while slipping them off knitting needle. Pull yarn to gather stitches and secure, then sew hat seam using mattress stitch.

Work embroidery next.

EMBROIDERY

Work embroidery using a blunt-ended yarn needle, one strand of yarn and lazy daisy stitch, straight stitch or French knots.

aran sweater

Quick to knit, this chunky cabled Aran sweater is a classic winter cover-up that would suit any little boy or girl. Knit it in this rich deep red or in your preferred shade.

SIZES & MEASUREMENTS

To fit

3–4	4–5	5–6	6–7	years

Knitted measurements

Around chest

66	71	76.5	82	cm
26	28	$30\frac{1}{4}$	$32\frac{1}{4}$	in

Length to shoulder

40	43	45	47	cm
$15\frac{3}{4}$	17	$17\frac{3}{4}$	$18\frac{1}{2}$	in

Sleeve length

28	30	32	34	cm
11	$11\frac{3}{4}$	$12\frac{3}{4}$	$13\frac{1}{4}$	in

YARN

9 (10: 11: 12) 50g/$1\frac{3}{4}$oz balls of Jaeger Extra Fine Merino Chunky in red/Red Ink 023 or desired shade

NEEDLES

Pair of $5\frac{1}{2}$mm (US size 9) knitting needles
Pair of 6mm (US size 10) knitting needles
Cable needle

TENSION/GAUGE

15 sts and 20 rows to 10cm/4in measured over st st using 6mm (US size 10) needles.

ABBREVIATIONS

See page 9.

BACK

Using 5½mm (US size 9) needles, cast on 66 (70: 74: 78) sts.

Rib row 1 (RS) *K2, P2, rep from * to last 2 sts, K2.

Rib row 2 *P2, K2, rep from * to last 2 sts, P2.

Rep last 2 rows twice more, ending with a WS row.

Change to 6mm (US size 10) needles and beg cable patt as foll:

Row 1 (RS) P6, K10, P2 (3: 4: 5), K8, P2 (3: 4: 5), K10, P2 (3: 4: 5), K8, P2 (3: 4: 5), K10, P6.

Row 2 (WS) K6, P10, K2 (3: 4: 5), P8, K2 (3: 4: 5), P10, K2 (3: 4: 5), P8, K2 (3: 4: 5), P10, K6.

Row 3 Rep row 1.

Row 4 Rep row 2.

Row 5 P6, K10, P2 (3: 4: 5), C4F, C4B, P2 (3: 4: 5), K10, P2 (3: 4: 5), C4F, C4B, P2 (3: 4: 5), K10, P6.

Row 6 Rep row 2.

Row 7 P6, C10F, P2 (3: 4: 5), K8, P2 (3: 4: 5), C10F, P2 (3: 4: 5), K8, P2 (3: 4: 5), C10F, P6.

Row 8 Rep row 2.

Row 9 Rep row 1.

Row 10 Rep row 2.

Row 11 Rep row 5.

Row 12 Rep row 2.

(These 12 rows are repeated to form cable patt.)

Work 28 (30: 32: 34) rows more in cable patt, ending with a WS row; a total of 40 (42: 44: 46) patt rows have been completed.

Shape armholes

Keeping patt correct as set, dec 1 st at each end of next row.

Work straight/even for 1 row.

Dec 1 st at each end of next row.**

Work straight/even for 33 (35: 37: 39) rows, ending with a WS row; a total of 76 (80: 84: 88) patt rows have been completed.

Shape right neck edge and shoulder

Next row (RS) Work first 18 (19: 20: 21) sts in patt, then turn, leaving rem sts on a stitch holder.

Work on these 18 (19: 20: 21) for right side of neck.

Dec 1 st at beg of next row (neck edge).

Cast/bind off 5 (5: 6: 6) sts at beg of next row and dec 1 st at end of same row.

Cast/bind off 5 (6: 6: 6) sts at end of next row. Rejoin yarn and cast/bind off rem 6 (6: 6: 7) sts.

Shape left neck edge and shoulder

With RS facing, slip centre 26 (28: 30: 32) sts onto another stitch holder, then rejoin yarn and work last 18 (19: 20: 21) sts in patt. Complete as for right side, reversing shaping.

FRONT

Work as for back to **.

Work straight/even for 21 (23: 25: 27) rows, ending with a WS row; a total of 64 (68: 72: 76) patt rows have been completed.

Shape left neck edge and shoulder

Next row (RS) Work first 24 (25: 26: 27) sts in patt, then turn, leaving rem sts on a stitch holder.

Work on these 24 (25: 26: 27) sts for left side of neck.

Dec 1 st at neck edge on next 4 rows, ending with a RS row.

Work straight/even for 1 row.

Dec 1 st at neck edge on next row and 3 foll alt

rows, ending with a RS row.

Work straight/even for 1 row.

Cast/bind off 5 (5: 6: 6) sts at beg of next row (shoulder edge).

Cast/bind off 5 (6: 6: 6) sts at end of next row.

Rejoin yarn and cast/bind off rem 6 (6: 6: 7) sts.

Shape right neck edge and shoulder

With RS facing, slip centre 14 (16: 18: 20) sts onto another stitch holder, then work last 24 (25: 26: 27) sts in patt.

Complete as for left side, reversing shaping.

SLEEVES (make 2)

Using 5½mm (US size 9) needles, cast on 42 (42: 44: 44) sts.

Rib row 1 (RS) K2 (2: 1: 1), *P2, K2, rep from * to last 4 (4: 3: 3) sts, P2, K2 (2: 1: 1).

Rib row 2 P2 (2: 1: 1), *K2, P2, rep from * to last 4 (4: 3: 3) sts, K2, P2 (2: 1: 1).

Rep last 2 rows 3 times more.

Change to 6mm (US size 10) needles and beg cable patt as foll:

Row 1 (RS) P6 (5: 5: 4), K8, P2 (3: 4: 5), K10, P2 (3: 4: 5), K8, P6 (5: 5: 4).

Row 2 (WS) K6 (5: 5: 4), P8, K2 (3: 4: 5), P10, K2 (3: 4: 5), P8, K6 (5: 5: 4).

Row 3 Rep row 1.

Row 4 Rep row 2.

Row 5 P into front and back of first st, P5 (4: 4: 3), C4F, C4B, P2 (3: 4: 5), K10, P2 (3: 4: 5), C4F, C4B, P5 (4: 4: 3), P into front and back of last st. 44 (44: 46: 46) sts.

Row 6 K7 (6: 6: 5), P8, K2 (3: 4: 5), P10, K2 (3: 4: 5), P8, K7 (6: 6: 5).

Row 7 P7 (6: 6: 5), K8, P2 (3: 4: 5), C10F, P2 (3: 4: 5), K8, P7 (6: 6: 5).

Row 8 Rep row 6.

Row 9 Rep row 7.

Row 10 Rep row 6.

Row 11 P into front and back of first st, P6 (5: 5: 4), C4F, C4B, P2 (3: 4: 5), K10, P2 (3: 4: 5), C4F, C4B, P6 (5: 5: 4), P into front and back of last st. 46 (46: 48: 48) sts.

Row 12 K8 (7: 7: 6), P8, K2 (3: 4: 5), P10, K2 (3: 4: 5), P8, K8 (7: 7: 6).

(These 12 rows are repeated to form cable patt.)

Cont in cable patt as set and at the same time inc 1 st at each end of 5th row and then every foll 6th row until there are 56 (58: 60: 62) sts, taking inc sts into rev st st at sides of cable panel and ending with a RS row; a total of 41 (47: 47: 53) patt rows have been completed. Work straight/even in patt for 5 (3: 7: 5) rows, ending with a WS row; a total of 46 (50: 54: 58) patt rows have been completed.

Shape top of sleeve

Keeping patt correct as set, cast/bind off 3 sts at beg of every row until 14 (16: 18: 20) sts rem. Cast/bind off in patt.

TO FINISH

Do NOT press.

Sew right shoulder seam.

Neckband

With RS facing and using 5½mm (US size 9) needles, pick up and knit 11 sts down left front neck edge, knit 14 (16: 18: 20) sts from centre front neck stitch holder, pick up and knit 10 sts up right front neck edge, pick up and knit 2 sts down right back neck edge, knit 26 (28: 30: 32) sts from centre back neck stitch holder, pick up and knit 3 sts up left back neck edge. 66 (70: 74: 78) sts.

Next row (WS) *P2, K2, rep from * to last 2 sts, P2.

Next row *K2, P2, rep from * to last 2 sts, K2.

Rep last 2 rows twice more, ending with a RS row.

Cast/bind off in rib.

Weave in all loose ends.

Sew left shoulder seam and neckband seam.

Fold top of each sleeve in half to find centre and mark with a pin.

Sew sleeves to armholes, matching centre top of sleeve to shoulder seam.

Sew side and sleeve seams.

cable scarf

Make this scarf in your favourite colour for a special child. You can knit it any length you like. The one shown here is extra-long and wraps several times around the neck for snuggly warmth.

SIZE

Finished scarf measures approximately 23cm/9in wide by 130cm/51in long (or adjust to desired length), excluding fringe.

YARN

Five 50g/1¾oz balls of Jaeger Baby Merino DK in orange/Orange 234 or desired shade

NEEDLES

Pair of 4mm (US size 6) knitting needles
Cable needle

TENSION/GAUGE

22 sts and 30 rows to 10cm/4in measured over st st using 4mm (US size 6) needles.

ABBREVIATIONS

See page 9.

SPECIAL YARN NOTE

If you want to make the scarf as long as possible without running out of yarn for the fringe, cut all the lengths of yarn for the fringe before beginning the scarf (see end of instructions).

TO MAKE SCARF

Using 4mm (US size 6) needles, cast on 78 sts.

Row 1 (RS) K3, [P3, K20] 3 times, P3, K3.

Row 2 K6, [P20, K3] twice, P20, K6.

Rows 3 and 4 Rep rows 1 and 2.

Row 5 K3, P3, K20, P3, C10B, C10F, P3, K20, P3, K3.

Row 6 Rep row 2.

Rows 7–10 Rep rows 1 and 2 twice.

Row 11 K3, P3, C10B, C10F, P3, K20, P3, C10B, C10F, P3, K3.

Row 12 Rep row 2.

Rows 1–12 form cable patt.

Rep rows 1–12 rows until scarf measures approximately 130cm/51in from cast-on edge or desired length, ending with a patt row 2 or 8 (a WS row).

Cast/bind off in patt on RS.

TO FINISH

Do NOT press scarf.

Fringe

For each fringe tassel, cut four 40cm/16in lengths of yarn.

Hold four strands together and fold in half. Then draw folded end through a stitch at one corner on one end of scarf, using a crochet hook. Pull all eight tail-ends of tassel through loop at folded end and tighten firmly to form a knot.

Attach a total of 17 fringe tassels across each end of scarf in same way, spacing them evenly apart. Trim fringe to 14cm/5½in long or desired length.

cable and lace poncho

Make this pretty cable and lace poncho for a little girl who needs an extra layer to keep warm during those cold winter months. It combines traditional stitch patterns and a modern silhouette.

SIZES & MEASUREMENTS

To fit 3–4 (4–5: 5–6: 6–7) years

Knitted measurements

The poncho is made up of two knitted rectangular panels, each measuring 28.5 (31: 33.5: 37)cm/11¼ (12¼: 13¼: 14½)in wide by 51.5 (54.5: 57.5: 60.5)cm/20¼ (21½: 22¾: 23¾)in long.

YARN

5 (5: 6: 6) 50g/1¾oz balls of Jaeger Baby Merino DK in bright pink/Lolly 229 or desired shade

NEEDLES

Pair of 4mm (US size 6) knitting needles

Cable needle

TENSION/GAUGE

22 sts and 30 rows to 10cm/4in measured over st st using 4mm (US size 6) needles.

ABBREVIATIONS

See page 9.

PONCHO PANELS (make 2)

Using 4mm (US size 6) needles, cast on 85
(91 : 97 : 103) sts.

Work 5 rows in garter st (K every row) for
border.

Beg cable and lace patt as foll:

Row 1 (WS) K4, *P8, K2 (3 : 4: 5), P11, K2 (3: 4:
5), rep from * twice more, P8, K4.

Row 2 (RS) K2, P2, *K8, P2 (3: 4: 5), K1, yf, K3,
sk2p, K3, yf, K1, P2 (3: 4: 5), rep from * twice
more, K8, P2, K2.

Row 3 and all foll WS (odd-numbered) rows
Rep row 1.

Row 4 K2, P2, *K8, P2 (3: 4: 5), K2, yf, K2,
sk2p, K2, yf, K2, P2 (3: 4: 5), rep from * twice
more, K8, P2, K2.

Row 6 K2, P2, *C8F, P2 (3: 4: 5), K3, yf, k1,
sk2p, K1, yf, K3, P2 (3: 4: 5), rep from * twice
more, C8F, P2, K2.

Row 8 K2, P2 * K8, P2 (3: 4: 5), K4, yf, sk2p,
yf, K4, P2 (3: 4: 5), rep from * twice more, K8,
P2, K2.

(These 8 rows are repeated to form cable and
lace patt.)

Rep rows 1–8 until panel measures
50:53:56:59cm/19¾ (21: 22: 23¼)in from
cast-on edge, ending with a WS row.

Work 5 rows in garter st for border, ending
with a RS row.

Cast/bind off purlwise.

TO FINISH

Do NOT press.

Pin cast-on edge of first panel to a row-end
edge of second panel, aligning right row-end
edge of first panel with cast/bound-off edge
of second panel, and sew in place.

Pin cast-on edge of second panel to a row-end
edge of first panel, aligning right row-end
edge of second panel with cast/bound-off
edge of first panel, and sew in place.

Index

Acknowledgements

The publishers would like to thank
Amber, Anish, Bo, Dylan, Eva, Izabella, Jade, Jessica,
Luca, Rachel and Zac for being such wonderful models

Executive Editor Katy Denny
Editor Emma Pattison
Executive Art Editor Penny Stock
Senior Production Controller Manjit Sihra
Photographer Janine Hosegood
Pattern Checker Stella Smith